Falling Back
in Love Again

12 Steps To Saving Your Relationship

THIRD EDITION

DR. DAVID R.L.
STEVENS

FALLING BACK IN LOVE AGAIN:
12 Steps To Saving Your Relationship
THIRD EDITION

Copyright © 2024 **Dr. David R.L. Stevens**

ISBN (Paperback): 978-1-964494-87-6
ISBN (Ebook): 978-1-964494-88-3

Printed in the United States of America.

PROMINENT
BOOKS

5830 E 2nd St, Ste 7000 #9983
Casper, WY 82609
USA

To order additional copies of this book, contact:
https://drstevenssoundmarriages.com/

Orders @Amazon / Kindle or order this book by author and title from:
Sound Marriage Ministry c/o Christ Center Church of God
1615-19 W. Chelten Ave. Philadelphia, PA 19126
215-548-7483 ccenter22cog@gmail.com

CONTENTS

FOREWORD

Listen, my wife and I have personally been happily married for over 60 years. We have been successfully counseling couples for more than 50 of those years. There are hundreds of marriages still holding together that have used the stuff my wife and I have used, and are healthy and well! I have had the privilege to author now this 9th book about marriage and family relationships. Over the course the many years we have produced video series, done numerous radio interviews, written many articles on the subjects of marriage, and healthy relationships, led numerous national and local seminars and conferences on these same topics. Not too long ago it was our unplanned pleasure to sit down at a graduation luncheon where we discovered, not only the honoree and her spouse, but there were 4 other couples who were mentored and married by me. The longest married couple at that event was happy to say it had been 37 years for them. So, my conclusion is that *I do have something very worthwhile to say!* **Are you ready to listen?**

CHAPTER 1

A Perfect Marriage

SHELLEY ASKED ME, **"What is a perfect marriage?"** I had to pause and think for a long while. I thought of Dan and Trumain, who have been married forever. They finish each other's sentences. They also like what each other likes and find each other's jokes funny. Then, I thought of Frank and Della who are as cool as cool can be. They seemingly float along through life undaunted by very much that comes their way. They are committed to God, each other, and their kids. Then there is Rick and Fawn, longtime partners, who are committed to the Lord, but who have endured a long history with medical problems, but yet their anchor holds. Jorge and Ada, though they were not married as long as Rick and Fawn, but even through their medical challenges, still held steadfastly to their marriage.

When I think about each of these couples and the individuals that make up these twosomes, they're all so different. They differ in character, disposition, and in many other ways. The Pauls' are delightful but very different in personalities. He is somewhat tentative about things and she is secure and opinioned. Still they are always able to reach a happy middle ground in their decision-making. The Caldwell's are not publicly gushy, but their love and devotion to each other cannot be questioned. He is the rock of the family. When he speaks, everybody listens. Della 's easy smile lets you know that she is at ease with her husband's gentle leadership. They don't fuss, they don't fight! On the other hand, Carl and Patty challenge each other on everything. If he says yes, she is probably going to say no. But let no one think that they are not deeply in love. When it comes down to it, they adore each other.

So how do we define real love? Also, what is the perfect marriage? What may be perfect to one couple may be rather stressful to another. I think there are many happy couples, who are pretty comfortable with each other, causing them to be settled in their relationships. So, "perfect marriage" may be a rather relative term.

In a previous book I said that the strongest thing that we have going for us is our will. The will is not an organ, but all the organs respond to it. Whatever one determines to do it is very likely to be done. No wonder, the great power emanating from the Bible passage presented in Philippians 4:8. It literally thunders! *"Whatever things that are true, whatever things are honest, whatever things are just, whatever things are pure, whatever things are lovely, whatever things are of good report; if there be any virtue and if there be any praise, think on these things."* Yes, **"Think on these things!"** Think on these things that really matter like truth, honesty, justice, purity, loveliness, and on all things that give a good report.

As a marriage counselor, I would rather encourage people to forget about trying to have a perfect marriage and strive to be perfectly married. The latter goal works toward settling and narrowing the scope. What I have is what I have! There is no need to look out to find anything else. When you believe that your spouse is perfectly suited to meet your needs, looking outside is not even an option.

I think that this may be a major factor in why some people cheat. They refused to close the door on their relationship; instead they look for a gap-filler. That's a person who came along and painted a fantasy that seemed to look like they are supplying something that's missing. This is how so many couples get into trouble. Instead of concentrating on what they have, they concentrate and pine away on what they think they don't have. That's how the devil gets into the mix. Trust me if your relationship finds an anchor in the Spirit of God, you actually have everything you need in a spouse. What you don't have is what you don't need. Remember a want is not a need!

The Rev. Dawes found so many things to complain about concerning his wife that it was not long before his gap—filler showed up. The other woman seemed to him to be everything that was missing in his wife Mary. So, he dumped Mary and went after the gap-filler. Two years later, history was on the move again. Could it be that there were a few things wrong with the good reverend? The gap-filler was his lack of determination to settle. If a person fixes their mind on negative stuff, what else is going to be the outcome?

Remember, your will plays an important role in what follows thereafter. It sets the policy, tone, direction, and determination. My wife and I personally stood over 50 years ago at the marriage altar with our wills set on having a great marriage. In so doing, we determined to do the work involved. Moreover, I like Dr. Charles Myrick's challenge given to the vast audience of the National Association of the Church of God, "Catch the vision—join the work!" There is indeed a lot of work to do to make the vision come true. New couples should develop a vision, set goals, and be determined to march to a victorious marriage. Fix your minds from the beginning that this will be a joyous marriage!

Roger and Buenita have been married for a long time. Their marriage in the 1960s raised some eyebrows. Roger is not an African-American but Buenita his adoring wife is. They loved each other from the very start and were determined to love each other no matter what. They made up their minds that their vision for a good life together was worth all the efforts it would take. Sure, because life is life, they have had ups and downs, but they never lost sight of the prize.

They chose, back in those days, to settle down in a state that discouraged mixed racial marriages. Because of that decision they did face some adversities, but God prevailed. Through it all they remained determined, even to this day, they still love each other no matter what they have experienced!

Let me make this strong point here about falling back in love: In order to get back to a burning love, we have to start remembering the innocent, first days of love. This is the beginning place to rekindle a romance. Very few people enter into marriage without feeling some kind of romantic love. I say very few, because, there are certainly a few situations that skip romance altogether. But for the most part, most people started their journey with some form of romance.

One exception would be Stanshaska and JoPal who were promised by their parents to each other since their infancy. The agreement between their parents was for them to wed at the age of 19. During the growing up years, the two children hardly knew each other. Since they lived in separate, villages it would be better said that they knew of each other before the actual ceremony. All they really knew was that they had been promised to each other. In their cultural tradition, there was no room for any questions or discussion. It had been all arranged and they were expected to go along with the program. This probably would not happen in our Western culture unless; these folks were living in one of the small subcultural groups that operated according to a tradition outside of what we consider the norm.

Another exception would be a throwback from many years ago whereas numerous couples were forced to marry because the woman was pregnant. It did not matter whether they really loved each other or not. The shame of it would not be tolerated. This forced nuptial was known rather unaffectionately as, "a shotgun wedding." It still happens today, but not as much because of our relaxed societal morals about such things, and certainly, and sadly, the availability of abortions. Unfortunately, abortion has become like an eraser on the end of the pencil.

About the same time that abortions were on the rise there was a brief shift in the trend. Liberal media aired the Murphy Brown TV program, featuring a single career woman seeking a sperm donor. This, according to the script, was to prevent permanent involvement or attachment to a man. Former Vice President Dan Quail spoke out in 1992 about the programs' brazen attempt to go against the traditional, societal, norm of a two-parent marital union. Vice President Quail found out he was like a salmon swimming upstream. Unlike the salmon, Quail was stopped short in his journey to uphold traditional

Christian values. In fact, his comments were viewed as so outlandish, and out of touch by a liberal hostile media that he was struck out with one swing from his possible run for a presidential candidacy. The Murphy Brown affair was the launching of a whole new public attitude for women seeking to raise babies without the children having fathers. This was just a little social history, a little far of field, but it came to mind when I thought of situations where romance is taken away or missing from what normally would be a love connection. So, in most normal situations there has to be some sort of romantic spark that will cause nuptials to bloom.

If in most normal situations, a marital relationship starts with romantic love, I think this is a good place to rekindle. My premise is that falling back in love has a lot to do with using those early pleasant memories of how one's love began. Being able to go back in time capturing moments of bliss and pleasure are qualified by our Philippians 4:8 Scripture construction, **"...think on these things."**

The best way to keep love alive is to feed it! Anything allowed to starve will die. If you think of a fire in an outdoor grill, as long as you keep adding charcoal briquettes, it will probably keep on cooking. The grease from the meat also helps to keep it going. When you're no longer grilling and the fatty juices are no longer dripping, the fire begins to wane away. It is just reality; if not attended to, the flames will die. Notice however, for a while the flames can be rekindled back to life by applying a slow gentle stream of air to the embers. *(kind of reminiscent of how The Holy Spirit works in our lives.)* If we continue fanning the embers, they will come alive again, but more fuel needs to be added. If the fire is allowed to go completely out, then the only remedy is to start the fire over again. If the grill master wants to continue cooking more food and there is a dead fire, there is no debate; the fire must be started again. The ashes may have to be emptied and perhaps new briquettes added, but again there is no debate that you'll have to start the fire again! If your love has gone cold, there should be no delay and no debate, ***START THE FIRE AGAIN!***

FOR YOUR NOTES & REFLECTIONS

....

....

....

....

....

....

....

....

....

....

....

....

....

....

CHAPTER 2

Falling Back in Love All Over Again

WHAT REALLY MADE you fall in love in the first place? Go back in time; reminiscence on the things that caused you to be attracted to the one you fell in love with. Remember, time erases or changes some things and you will never be able to recapture 100% of everything. But let's try for the moment to go back in time. If Susan weighed 125 pounds 10 years ago when you met her and has gained 25 pounds since then; it may not be feasible to picture her minus the extra pounds. But think how she made you feel when you were with her 10 years ago. That's what I'm talking about; that's where I'm trying to take you. What were some of the places you have visited together? What did you talk about? What were some of the things that made you laugh? This actually falls right in line again with Philippians chapter 4 verse 8 which encourages us to *think on positive things.* There is another Scripture (Proverbs 5:18) that tells us men (or women) to *rejoice in the wife* (or husband) *of your youth.* This Scripture, just like the Philippians 4 reference, is dealing with *how we structure our thoughts.* To add one more scriptural reference for this time: Proverbs 23:7 paraphrased, "as a man/woman thinks in their heart so is he/she." A lot of who you are starts in your heart/mind.

If you think of yourself as a person who is very grateful to God for placing you where you are, and giving you what you have, in all likelihood, you are going to make it. Gratefulness is a virtue!

I've found over these many years of living, studying, observing, experiencing things, and counseling people, that a lot of what we do and how we do it begins with what we think about it. Healthy thoughts will generally produce healthy actions. I said in my third book Marriage: Catching A Second Wind, *"First we say it, and then we do it!"* The thing that I would like to now add to that bit of wisdom is that the thought generates in our mind first! So, it might be better said: **"*First you think it,* and *then you say it*, and *then you go and do it!*"**

It is so extremely important that we engage in building back with positive stuff. You know those things that delighted us and turned us on, especially in those beginning times in the relationship. I remember from the personal beginning of our own relationship, a lot of humor surrounded us. Laughter back in the day was contagious and continues throughout the years of our joyful journey of marriage. My wife and I learned to find humor in life, even laughing at ourselves on many occasions.

We often laugh about my purchase of some bargain socks in our first year of marriage. I was finishing up my Senior year of college and money was tight. I went to this bargain store that stocked closeout items. I needed some socks and this bundle of several socks looked good. I went home thinking I had made a big score. The next morning, I was so excited to show off my thrifty purchase only to discover that my foot could only make it half way in. There was an unknown seam sewn across the inside, making it impossible to use. We discovered that all the socks in that bargain bundle were rejects. My trying to save money, turned out to be a waste of time, and money!

Thinking about a contrast to positive fun and laughter, there are people who speak negatively in almost every sentence. They seem to delight in telling you why something will not work? No matter what the plan is, they will see some failure in it. Bad enough with one person being that way, but it is really unfortunate when you have a negative couple. If you tell them there is a way that they can rekindle their sour relationship, they will say, "Not in a million years." They will give you 182 things that prevent this from happening. Beth and Henderson are like that, I know that they love each other although they have lived separately for many years. Whatever happened that caused their separation was so deep and hurtful, that neither is willing to take a risk at trying to solve it. Henderson suggested to me some time ago that they were better friends now than when they lived in the same space. How sad this is. They could be enjoying a full life as a married couple; instead they look forward to showing up at the same family functions not as a couple, how awkward. From time to time there are "How are you" phone calls and occasional business sessions that bring them together. They actually may love each other but just cannot get along for too long in the same space. I have discovered after years of trying to help folks like this that if they are not ready, they are not ready. If anything is to change for them, they have to go through the process of renewing and believing that all things are possible through Christ who strengthens us, and ultimately, He wants us to be happy with each other. But this has to be a serious heartfelt commitment to working it out. Yes, I do believe that God has a plan for our lives and will help us work that plan if we are willing to commit.

There is a simple premise that believes if someone has ever loved someone and something bad happens to cause a breach in that relationship, that love can be rekindled. It is strange, but we see it or hear about it all the time. A man treats his lady friend with callous disregard; yet, she keeps letting him come back. A woman leaves her husband and small children for another man and yet that husband has high hopes and regard that she'll come back. The genuine fires in the heart are often hard to extinguish and cancel out forever.

I think of these people who have been married more than once to the same person. What happened? They were first in love and something happened and then they declared that they were no longer in love and got a divorce. Then the embers sparked again and they were in love again. Some have even gone for a third term. The problem is that they could have worked it out without the termination the first time. Perhaps it would have been less costly to have engaged the services of a marriage counselor than the costs of remarriage/divorce. My point is that dying embers can revive and flourish. If they go out completely, they can be renewed by building the fire again.

Tell me, what are you passionate about? What turns you on? What is it you need in order to get your love box turned on again? Think honestly about this! Harlan and Tressa were high profile people who were dedicated to their careers. Somewhere along their journey they lost that flame. To be honest, they were committed to staying together loving each other for a lifetime, but it was more like duty than enjoyment. Let's face it love is not always burning red hot. We could compare it to our Philadelphia weather charts which go somewhat up, and somewhat down, but mostly in the middle with some spikes from time to time. Sometimes we have the sizzle and sometimes we almost have the fizzle. But it's up to us (paraphrased from Dr. Jesse Jackson) to *'keep love alive!'* "So good doctor how do you help these people? How do you help the couples who would like to get it settled so that they can have a solid reliable flame in their relationship?"

Well, my method for the high-profile couples would be almost the same as the couples facing normal pressures, except I would urge them to do this very important first step: GET YOUR BUSINESS OUT OF THE PRESS. Some of the failed celebrity marriages could have been saved if they had been wise enough to disregard the various divisive spins that media puts on them.

Elin and Tiger might have been able to reconcile if it had not gone against the desires of sharing their business with the press. Yes, Mr. Woods had some faithfulness problems to where publicly discovered he committed infidelity. But after he was caught for his adulterous affair, I think we saw a hidden side that we did not know was there. His arrogance diminished. It must have been a façade. Personally, I don't think his game would have suffered like it did if this thing did not really get to him. Sometimes we think of our sports champions and other people of prominence as if they were little tin gods who are bigger than life. The oil in a duck's feathers causes water to roll off of its' back. Tiger's oil was not able to keep his sins from penetrating his mind. Therefore, what was in his mind was troubling his physical game.

Moreover, there are many celebrities who have certainly been ruined by their bad behavior. Sadly, they're literally buried alive by the press, without a chance for marital redemption. It is almost like they take delight in finding hidden stuff that will initiate, justify, and provoke a breakup. Recently a gossip paper chose to announce that the Pinkett/Smiths were throwing in the towel, and divorce was imminent. Suddenly, the internet was abuzz with the news. The story turned out to be false, but the gossip sheet did not care. They kept maintaining that their sources were accurate, and because they trusted their sources they would not relent. They needed to be sued largely to be put permanently out of business; in my opinion, but that's just me! The reality is they stay in business because people buy Junk and easily fall for the lies!

Before any couple, celebrities, or just plain folks can move forward in a relationship where the embers are dead, or dying, especially if there has been infidelity, genuine repentance and then forgiveness must be expressed. Then repentance must be practiced. For some it is not too hard to say, but the talk must be the walk! This is a painful step for most people, but it cannot be swept away or sidetracked. There needs to be caution here when it comes to full discloser. Full discloser doesn't require intensive details. Repentance for what was done without filling out all of the glaring details of what was done. If the person, who cheated, sincerely repents, they will carry with them those past scars anyway even though they may fade but will not completely erase. There must be a willingness on the part of both individuals to *move away from what was, on to what can be! Yes,* **ON TO WHAT CAN BE!** Back to the question of how we move couples forward who are experiencing low fires or dying embers to a more comfortable hearth. My method is to get them going back in their minds to where it was good. Back to where it was fresh and exciting!

Back to the times when the flames were burning hot!

My question to Harland was what was it that excited you so much about Tressa? What was it that got the 'I can't help it's' or the 'I can't wait to get back to you Babe, going? Well this question certainly opened up the crayon box. He began to share some great memories of thrills and passions of the past. "Why did you stop doing these things?" I asked. The answer was pretty obvious. Life set in! Life has all of its responsibilities, time restraints, and daily juggling. Many couples fall into the trap of the 'same old same old.' It's so easy to fall into a pattern of everyday life and forget the things that brought pure joy. Often, they are the special little things that are done off of the regular beaten path. Sometimes, we allow ourselves to get so busy whereas we just don't make room for things off the beaten path. Our lives take on the regular routine, and we act as though we will fail if we allow any unplanned occurrences.

When I met with the Denison's' they told me how much fun they had traveling before the kids came. Now sadly they were tied to their jobs, kids, the PTA, the church, and the list goes on and on. I think what they were trying to tell me was that there was no time for having fun. "What about family vacations?" I asked. They've had some vacations and absolutely enjoyed them, but again timing was always crucial. The children were out of school for the summer, but it was hard to balance their camp schedules with the parents' vacation schedules. It seemed like time after time was followed with conflict after conflict. When I suggested not sending their three kids to camp this coming summer, and planning to focus on family fun things, they just looked at each other in wonderment. They had never ever thought of that. Enlightened smiles began to spread over their faces. Their expressions demonstrated that here was a plan that could work. It was early enough in the year that with careful planning and job cooperation they could really pull it off! From that moment on I think it was a done deal.

Family vacations are great, and so needed, but don't forget that Mommies and Daddies need together time too. Harland needed to have some fun time with Tressa!

Sometimes we get shackled to our routines and fall easily into believing that this is the only way it can be done. Usually, that's not true. We settle because it is normally just easier to settle. There is almost always a way to plan around the routine.

Once I remember teaching junior high school back in the 60s. What a coaster ride. Teaching and controlling kids, doing mountains of paperwork, endless faculty meetings, etc., I tell you how I was just overwhelmed. One day I realized that I was being choked alive by a pattern that provided no escapes. Why did I have to comply with all of that and feel so trapped? Well, all of those things did seem to be necessary for that time, but I decided to add one more thing that could make a difference. After school, instead of taking a 30-min. drive home through rush-hour traffic, I started visiting the music suites down in the underbelly of the school. It was there that I started to teach myself how to play the piano. I would go in one of the private rooms and just have the most fun for about an hour or more. When I finished, I had missed most of the rush-hour traffic and my arrival at home was always pleasant. The secret was I deliberately took time out to relax. Music transported me to a different place.

In many troubled marriages, there are no deliberate relaxing times. Stress upon stress is the order of the day. Things will not get better by themselves. One or in most cases both people must build meaningful downtime into the relationship. It will not happen by itself. You have to put it into place and be proactive! You have to set priorities that are going to help you.

I am currently counseling a couple that has very little meaningful quality time to spend with each other. They work different shifts. Yet, I discovered that they do spend the little time together watching late-night TV. They watch their favorite shows for several hours together until he falls asleep and has to get up for work. During these several hours they don't really converse on any important issues, they just laugh together. He tends to resent being awakened after getting just a few hours of inadequate sleep. She has to get him up to get to work at 5:30 AM. This is where the grumpiness comes out full force.

My simple solution: Get a video timing recorder to capture the televised programs and use half of the time to talk about important things and issues, and then go to bed and get the additional rest. Make your precious little time PRECIOUS! If TV together time is that important, pick a weekend time that does not jeopardize your relationship or your job.

Continuing our conversation about vacations and how important they are, let me make another point. Waiting and planning a one-time yearly vacation is not enough. A couple must try to get away often. Now every getaway does not have to be expensive. Overnighters away can often be for under $100. Watch the newspapers, magazines, and the Internet for hotel discounts. Sometimes you can find a special breakfast spot located in the hotel area if the regular hotel restaurant is too costly. Then there are some chains that offer continental breakfasts as part of the overnight stay. Usually these food offerings are not too bad. I remember one, or two of the chain restaurants that even provided eggs to order. Taking time to shop around can be beneficial to working with a tight budget. Do not use lack of money as an excuse. Don't make the mistake of saying, *"It* is too expensive," or *"It is out of our budget to do these getaways."* It is more than worth it to add value to your marriage. Some people are penny—wise and value-foolish! When you look back on the love investments, only the good that comes from it will be remembered. I don't think anyone will think back and remember how much money they had or didn't have and base their value on money. My dad's advice for keeping my new car running well for many years to come was, *"keep changing the oil in that car boy!"* I've tried to do that for each of my cars and been successful with each of them for many years above the manufacturers' guarantee. Oil in the car is like romance in the marriage. It is not the marriage, just like oil is not the car. The purpose of oil and romance is to cut down on the friction and keep the parts well-lubricated and running smoothly.

It is interesting to me how many of the couples that come to our relationship workshops and seminars are couples who actually are doing well in their marriages. Even though they are doing a great job they have decided to invest time and money into enhancing what they already have. In contrast to that, sometimes it seems we almost have to beg those with problematic relationships to invest (or admit they have a problem).

I recall one year when we were doing a big weekend at the Black Rock Conference Center in our area, we had a few cancellations. The rooms had been paid for and the couples could not come. We could not even give the rooms away to some who needed the experience. Now that's sad!

Listen if nothing else, you need time away. If during that time you can get some learning tools, it is a double blessing.

Then there are romantic things that you can do that cost no money: Try driving to a Lovers Lane (*these days with much concern for safety*). Almost every city, suburban, or rural area has one. Lovers Lane is a place where single people like to go to get their romance on. Because you are married, does not mean you have to miss out on the daring and the fun! Just be sure that safety is worked into all your plans.

When our kids were young and there was no one to babysit, we invented some fun times around camping out. We would use our living room as our place of intrigue. We had a kerosene heater, supplying the warmth and glow. We would sneak down stairs to our living room and make one sleeping bag out of our sheets and blankets. We would stay there enjoying our little romantic interlude all toasty and warm until the early morning hours, and then sneak up to our room. The children never knew what went on.

I've often thought about camping out in our back yard under the stars in good weather. But we haven't done this one yet.

If you have an empty nest, either permanently or occasionally, why not take full advantage of that time and unoccupied real estate? Dare to be free! Life is short. Why not enjoy as much romance as you can? Spice it up to suit yourselves! Make it your business; own it as your thing!

Source: Stevens, David. FALLING BACK IN LOVE: 7 Steps to saving your relationship (Kindle Locations 60288). David Stevens. Kindle Edition.

FOR YOUR NOTES & REFLECTIONS

....

....

....

....

....

....

....

....

....

....

....

....

....

....

CHAPTER 3

Bring Back the Romance

"CHILD, WE ARE *too old for that mushy stuff. We've been married for so long we don't need to go there anymore. I'm not going anywhere; he's not going anywhere. We are settled...!*" These words could have come from so many spouses.

On the other hand, I have some friends who are well into their 80s. For instance, one of my friends says when he sees me, "I'm still smiling." That was code between us about their sexual intimacy! We always had so much fun laughing about our little joke. While we were sharing our little fun time, sometimes his wife would come up and want to know what we were laughing about. We always kept our secret between us. I was shocked one day when she walked up and whispered in my ear, *"I'm still smiling too!"* Wow, she had cracked our secret code!

I like to use cars as object lessons, and here's another: you can buy a new car and drive it every day by only adding gasoline when needed. But the manufacturer recommends when to change the oil. You could ignore the instructions and even decide that since it came with oil you will just rely on what it came with. You just never take heed to the changing instructions because the car's performance is great. So, you continue to ride merrily along. There will come a time when the oil is burned and beaten into a disrespectful sludge. If you persist on ignoring all the warning signs that vehicle is going to one day cease up. Once I bought an old VW with a ceased engine from someone. I had no idea how hard it was going to be to find someone who knew how to fix it. I finally found one man who could free that engine. He really had to rebuild it. I learned from him that the only reason that this happens to an engine is a lack of oil. The motor will burn up, lock up, and just plain quit on you. If this happens with an automobile, it is sure to happen in a marriage relationship where there is no romance!

I'm sure you know people who have long since given up on *the mushy stuff* and are still together. Their commitment is fine, but it would be so much nicer to have some fun along the way!

The Greek word for romance is *Eros*. *Eros* is not sex. It is what you do to express love such as intimacy, if you are married. If a couple is not married, they have to be careful with romance. Unmarried couples need to be careful that they reach an appropriate cutoff point. One lecturer talked about the difficulties of establishing a permanent line with single daters. He felt that once a moral line had been crossed that it was near impossible to get this couple to retreat to a place below that breached line.

However, if we could get married people to recall and practice those romantic things that made their hearts pump faster when they dated; it would help keep love alive in their marital relationship. Remember it, then practice it! Bring those moments back to mind and work them for all they are worth!

I noticed the romantic pattern of one of our sons and his wife. It seemed like every time we look, they are finding some reason to go to the beach. Water has become their thing. It seems they have done this forever, and now they are implanting that same love for the ocean into their children. No doubt this will become a family tradition, but I am sure mom and dad will find ways to be alone too. Another example is one of our daughters and her husband seemed to know just about every small intimate restaurant in and out of town. This is a couple who will often take off and go for coffee before Sunday worship. I mentioned in another book that I saw them sitting in the dark church dining room early one Sunday morning sipping coffee together. It was too late for them to go to their regular spot so they turned this space and opportunity into a perfect romantic interlude. Both of these couples have found ways that they can recommend to others as places of reconnection. They have discovered and practice what we will call, *"Alone—time."*

Think about you two. What are some of the things you used to do together that just brought such a delight to the both of you?

Sometimes we get so busy with life and forget the little treasures that actually bring that personal joy.

Every couple should have these *"Alone times,"* or *"timeout moments"*. If you do not have them, then start creating them now! I borrowed insight from Gloria Gaither and Shirley Dobson's book title, *"Let's Make a Memory"*. Make pleasant memories and record them. Shirley and Gloria wanted us to journal memories in a lasting book of adventures, which is an excellent suggestion, but I urge you to record them on your mind as well. Someday, it may actually be a blessing to you as you revisit, in your mind those times of delight. It may even motivate a repeat!

Where are some of the simple places in life where the two of you have been together and had fun? Think of those places which seemed to turn you on! Personally, one of our first dates was at a drive-in theater in Anderson, Indiana. I was a student and quite broke. So, I did not have the money to go into the drive-in, but I knew a place where we could see the film from the outside. I don't think we could hear the sound, because of the distance, but in those days, you could figure out the plot pretty well without sound. Suddenly, it was like magic; while watching the movie, another drama occurred. All these *fireflies* or *lightning bugs,* appeared from nowhere. It looked like the whole valley between us and the giant screen was flooded with this mystical greenish yellow glow. Wow; Smile! Often, we mention that early time in our romance. When we think back on that event, perhaps that was a sign of our destiny! Praise God it has been more than a half of a happy century. We will talk more about that date in Chapter 7 **MEMORIES OLD and NEW.**

What are some of the simple pleasures that you have enjoyed together in the past that sparked such strong passions? Shirlease and Joe enjoyed making doughnuts together on Saturday mornings. They shared them with their Sunday school the next morning. Beatrice and Ron enjoyed quiet walks together on the country roads around their home.

Ted and Ursula enjoyed walking around the busy streets of their urban town house while pushing their twins in strollers. Jordan and Veronica are joggers. Somehow, they figured out a system that has her jogging while pushing a special baby stroller as Jordan jogs along holding the dog's leash. They reported having so much fun trying to negotiate this strange sight. Then there are the Kelly's who make it to the TV set at

11:30 PM every evening to hold hands and watch Nightline! Well to that I say, "Whatever turns you on (smile) turns you on!"

Romance can come in many forms and packages. Some things are simple, while some things are more elaborate. Cards and flowers are always nice. They usually signal that some extra care was taken. There's a story out there about former President Ronald Reagan who was battling Alzheimer's. He went out for a walk and was of course accompanied by the Secret Service. Mr. Reagan was clearly ailing from this illness as they walked along; when suddenly he turned and reached for the latch of an unfamiliar gate. Letting himself in he began to pick a beautiful flower. *"Mr. President,"* The Secret agent exclaimed, *"this is not our home." "Oh, I know..."* said Mr. Reagan. *"I just wanted to take my love a flower."* Even though he was thought to be mostly locked in a private world of his own, just for some few precious moments he returned to romantic thoughts of his precious Nancy, the love of his life! The embers of their love burned brightly in both of their hearts right through to the end of the former president's life.

Never underestimate the power of love and the importance of romance in that love. The Greek word Eros for romance is like the things you do to bring a type of lubrication to a situation. Pardon me, here I go again—*romance is like the oil in the motor that* **prevents friction which** **causes unwanted heat**. That unwanted heat would eventually destroy the engine.

Although the engine runs because of the fi re and combustion in its chambers, its parts must remain relatively cool and fluid as it goes about doing its work. If love is the outcome goal, the engine is the heart and mind. This combination engine is the driving force. Romance serves as the lubricant that keeps a fluid flow. That's why we have to be mindful of what we feed our heart and mind. Scripture teaches us that out of it will flow the issues of life.

On my very first teaching job, my wife placed a card in my lunch bag. I was not much of a card man at that time, but the sentiments on that card melted me! I kept the card and placed it in my desk drawer. Months later I rediscovered the envelope in the back of the drawer. I pulled it out and began to gush all over again. I actually had forgotten the words but again those same emotions reunited. I didn't think of myself as being a romantic type. She brought out a side of me that was new to me. This experience happened several times over the years until I went on to another assignment. Her act was more than a onetime event for me. Later I awakened to the fact that if Dorothy loves to send cards, she must love to receive them also. Dahhhh…the light came on!

One day I was driving home and I saw a florist shop. It occurred to me that Dot liked flowers. I only had about three dollars as I recall but I went in anyway. Kind of embarrassed, I asked the man if he had anything in my price range. Amazingly he came out with a beautiful little bouquet of common flowers.

As I brought them through the door, she was so excited. She loved them! We were really pinching pennies in those days, but she reacted as if I had brought her long stem roses or a box of orchids. For just three dollars I had made my bride extremely happy. It wasn't the money, but the thought that counted!

Later on, as I became somewhat more financially able, I discovered a lingerie shop in a little mall near where we lived. I went in to see if I could find Dot a gift one day. I looked around and a saleswoman came over. She asked what kind of gift I was looking for and the occasion? When I told her, there was no special occasion and that it was for my wife, she went crazy. She started calling all the other salesladies over to see this husband who was buying a 'Just-because gift' for his wife; Just because I love you. She explained that they were used to boyfriends coming in to get lingerie for their girlfriends, but never husbands for their own wives, unless it was some kind of make-up gift. That was so strange to me, what I was doing was not the norm? Wow! I had actually stumbled onto something unusually romantic. According to these women, something, many husbands were not practicing when it came to their own wives. Boyfriends were doing it, but apparently, many husbands were in this area, lacking.

Another tip that I learned for husbands, when buying lingerie, *make sure it's something that she will be comfortable with.* Don't buy skimpy stuff that's great eye candy for you. It should be something that is beautiful, but practical and comfortable.

A Thong or a G string might look sexually exciting to the husband but imagine how that must feel running down her rear end. Think also about this, lace may be pretty but if it comes in contact with her more sensitive body hairs you may want to rethink its purchase. Well anyway, these salesladies got to know me after a while as a frequent shopper. I was so sorry when they moved away. But have no fear; I discovered a replacement in the larger mall. Eventually they went out of business too so now I'm confined mostly to looking in the larger department store chains. My wife still appreciates me bring gifts, *"just because I love you"*. Most wives love lingerie, jewelry, and pretty things. But don't forget the small stuff like cards and flowers and balloons. Some like dolls and stuffed animals.

Many times, it's the little things that bring warm smiles and kisses.

Find those things that say, ***"Just because I love you!"***

One of the elements of being romantic is using the opportunity of surprise. Doing the unsuspected makes for some intriguing pleasures. Doing those minuscule things that make happy memories is important. One cold Friday I picked my wife up from her school like I normally would. Instead of driving toward home I took a different route heading out of town. To throw her off, I gave some vague information about wanting to show her something or other. In about a half of an hour we pulled into an advertised love retreat that I had booked for an overnight stay. In the trunk of the car I had packed a small suitcase. She was so surprised, and of course very delighted. After checking in, we went to a romantic dinner. Finally, when we were back in our room, it was all that it was promised to be. The hot tub*, fireplace, candles, apple cider and all were wonderful. The next morning when we peered out of our window it had snowed. The crackle of the logs in the fireplace fit the occasion.

That certainly was a weekend to remember. I actually got the information about the love nest from a single female colleague who learned that I was looking for a special place to surprise my wife. Sometimes single folks have romantic knowledge that they will share because they think what you are trying to do is so cool. Don't be afraid to check them out for ideas; they may prove to be a wealth of information, and inspiration.

All of the above is good for the non-occasion, occasions, but let me share another clue: **never forget celebration dates**. Birthdays and anniversaries are special occasions that must be remembered and celebrated before we can talk about doing the extra things. I know someone who in their fairly long marriage,

---

*   I mentioned that the hot tub was a romantic thing to do, but in light of all the various strains of viruses and diseases, caution should be taken when using any things shared with the public. I know nowadays my wife likes to spray hotel bedding with Lysol disinfectant. She also likes to use disinfectant hand wipes on all hard surfaces. I know you cannot do everything in the world to be safe, and there is no written guarantee. But we should do as much as we can to ensure our health and safety.

still continues to struggle with dates. There is very little excuse these days because of all of the electronic gadgets available to alert us, etc. For the extra to count the most, the regular/normal must be celebrated first. This includes the regular doing and helping with chores and duties in the home. Then when the *just because I love you'* comes along it means so much more!

Benjamin kept forgetting to get gifts and cards to celebrate the actual date of his wife's birthday. He tried to buy her something within a certain range of dates, usually after the fact, really pointing out that he was fishing for the right date. He just could not remember. This always of course took a little of the joy out of the celebration. Benjamin, listen to me, **_"write it down"_**!

Post it somewhere if you have to! If you don't have a mind for detail, it's okay to write stuff down so you won't forget!

Being romantic takes work and planning. Everyone is not a spontaneous romantic. If being romantic does not come naturally to you, get the help you need. Talk to your friends, find out what they are doing; or find out things they've done in the past, or romantic things they have heard about. If they can share one thing that you can include in your arsenal of things to do, then you are ahead of the game. You can become a collector of ideas. You don't always have to reinvent the wheel. Collect ideas from newspapers and magazines articles, etc. You can also get ideas from TV and the internet. Just be careful with things you see and get from any of these media sources because some come without any kind of moral standard. I am not big on any suggestions that hint of any kind of public exposure and the possibility of moral embarrassment. A Christian does not ever want to get caught up in anything that would bring any shame to the God we serve. Try to make wholesome selections around things that your partner would want and be comfortable with. Exercising selfishness can become a turnoff.

Remember married people, **romance is an expression of love!** *Think of it as a vehicle transporting you somewhere.* **Sexual intimacy does not always have to be the goal, or the field goal!** *It certainly should be at times, but you should not withhold from being romantic only for those times that you can be sexual.* Don't forget the regular practice of sensual touching. A casual brush by, a provocative rear end pat or squeeze, a gentle peck on the neck, even a luscious body squeeze, and a daring occasional surprise erogenous zone touch, add a lot of hot romance to married life. Being a regular romantic will certainly help you in those times when full sexual expression can fully be satisfied in a time of intercourse.

Romance—REMEMBER IT IS CUMULATIVE! I love the principle of deposits and withdrawals introduced by Dr. Stephen Covey. When you make deposits, you will have the ability to make withdrawals later on. You cannot expect to make withdrawals that exceed your deposits. My simple conclusion is that, *'Romance is work! But it is always a work in progress. Great dividends will follow. This makes it cumulative.'*

FOR YOUR NOTES & REFLECTIONS

....

....

....

....

....

....

....

....

....

....

....

....

....

....

CHAPTER 4

Break Up to Make Up?

THERE IS AN interesting philosophy out there that is shared by many relationship counselors. These counselors tend to believe that it's okay for married spouses having serious issues with each other, to physically separate in their living arrangements. In other words, if you're not getting along—then go along by yourself. Only in cases where there is either instances of physical abuse, or the threat of such, would I agree with this philosophy. I believe that it is better to stay together and work out your differences than to try and negotiate from a distance.

If you examine the chapters on LOCKING DOORS and MEMORIES OLD AND NEW you will see that I am very careful about what we place in our minds. Let's say for instance, couple A argues over not having adequate money for bills and the wife decides to spend money that they did not have in the first place, for a new dress. Husband A gets so mad that he says some very intimidating and character assassinating things. This in turn angers and irritates his wife to no good end. So, wife A on the advice of a friend leaves, her home without notice, to stay with a fellow worker for a few days.

After the few days are up, wife A resurfaces. All the time during her absence husband A has been frantically searching for her. What started out as a fundamental disagreement based on their lack of money, and the spending thereof, was allowed to escalate into a more major problem than needed. Their tempers took them to another place entirely. Insulting, demeaning words were hurled. Inappropriate decisions and actions followed, and the original dilemma was buried in what grew out from it.

In essence, the responses to the original problem took it to a new level of conflict. Not only is wife A accused of being insensitive to their lack of money, but on top of that she is labeled with some bad words describing her intelligence and her motivation. Not only is husband A over reacting to his wife's spending, but also establishes himself as a bully who is insensitive to his wife's feelings. All of this is certainly bad enough, but on top of that in thinking about reconciliation a brand-new problem emerges. So, when we confront the actual financial problem and what might be a poor decision to spend money that they did not have, or at least did not have to spend, husband A blurts out, *"but you left me, and that was not fair"*.

Herein lies a deeper problem. What started out as a spending problem, quickly took on deeper implications. Even though husband A was wrong for his insensitive bullying, it is hard for him to get over the fact that she left him. Words like abandonment and defection become indelibly painted on his mind.

My wife has a simple, uncomplicated statement that will help many couples who are trying to put the marriage cart back up on its wheels. ***"Don't do negative to try and get positive"***. Her wisdom is so simple but astounding. Dorothy has cut through all of the possible debate, with her ***"Don't do negative things in order to try to bring about positive solutions"***.

In an actual case where Laura stormed out of the house because of an argument with her husband Powell, the scars ran deeply. Laura, a middle age woman who had never been married, was living with her parents when she met Powell. After a very short courtship they were married. They settled down together in a little town that was not too far from her hometown. Both people experienced difficulty blending their relationship because both were pretty set in their ways. Their biggest problem was they just plain did not understand each other and the way they thought about life and how to approach it. This lack of understanding caused them to scrap about most everything. One day Laura got so upset with Powell that she, without warning, packed up her things and left their home. When Powell returned home from work, he found most of her personal things gone. He frantically called around to see if anyone knew of her whereabouts. No one seemed to know. He even called the local hotels in town, thinking she might have taken asylum there. But all of his efforts brought no satisfaction. Finally, he decided reluctantly, to call her parents to report her missing and to ask for their help in finding her. It was quite a shock to him to find that he had to search no further. Laura had returned back to her parents' house, and they had willingly allowed her to return. Having a good relationship with her family, and especially her parents, he never expected that they would not try to communicate with him.

So now not only is there a problem existing with Laura, but now there is a family divide. His love and trust for her family is now in question. He had not abused her or mistreated her in anyway. Sure, there were arguments and disagreements, but pretty much run-of-the-mill disagreements. Nothing earth shaking.

Powell now felt betrayed by her parents. He had thought of them being his mom and dad since both of his parents were deceased. On the phone he hears the voice of her father now lashing out at him without even regarding that there might be another side to the story. What began with the couple as a poor communication problem and a serious lack of understanding, now has turned into a miniature war zone with unwitting soldiers lining up in support of one person or another. The more time away from each other, the more collective mess accumulated. Powell began to have thoughts that maybe Laura moved out to be closer to this man next door to her parents. They had dated for a long period of time, but he had never gotten up the gumption to propose. It was widely known that they had had affections for each other. This man's name had surfaced a few times too many in her conversations with Powell.

Laura, while separated from her husband, began to remember the cute little woman who was quite single, living in the house in back of them. She saw the way this woman flirted with her husband while she was hanging out her wash. "Who does that anymore", Laura wondered? Everybody in this development has a clothes dryer. It seemed to her, every time Powell was in their backyard, doing barbecue, this woman would show up with wet clothes, and a conversation. The green-eyed monster was certainly now awake, and fully active in her mind!

Look at the number of suspicions, innuendos, and distractions that have occurred because of a lack of understanding, and an unwillingness to deal with perhaps one thing. This careless decision has now mushroomed into something much larger. I wish Dorothy could have had the chance to share her wisdom, ***"Don't do negative to try and get positive"***.

So, you can see, I have a fundamental disagreement with the theory and practice, of breaking up to make up. ***Again, let me affirm that if there is any danger, physical fighting, uncontrollable anger taking the form of unwanted physical behavior, etc. I say <u>run as far and as fast as you can</u> to put distance between the two of you!*** And also let me say this, most of the time when we think of staving off physical abuse, we are thinking of protecting the woman. Let me assure you it is not always the woman who is physically abused. I am aware of instances where husbands have been violently attacked, dismembered, wrongly accused of violence, and incarcerated because of false accusations. Marriage should be based on equal love and trust. Equal love and trust is not just something that is talked about. It must be demonstrated!

Demonstration is required by both spouses.

Even in settling our differences, love and trust must be demonstrated! Because I love my wife, I am careful how I treat my defenses of those matters that differ from what she believes. Even when I believe what I am defending, or what I am presenting, makes more sense to me, I must remember not to demean or belittle her opinion. I respect her and must be intentional about showing that respect at all times. Even in those times when debate and rebuttal might reach a heated level. **After all is said and done love must stand strong!**

I always like to balance my comments with biblical structure. If we would discipline our behavior according to God's behavior manual, the Bible, we would certainly avoid things like **'Breakup to make up'**. In *Ephesians 4 vs. 25–27* we find this sage advice:

25 Therefore, putting away lying, "Let each one of you speak truth with his neighbor," for we are members of one another. 26 "Be angry, and do not sin": do not let the sun go down on your wrath, 27 nor give place to the devil.

I see these biblical passages as five strong principles in the management of conflicts, especially relating them to marital conflict. Let's spend some time looking at them in this light.

"Let each one of *you speak truth with his neighbor*," your neighbor in this instance would be your spouse. In order to deal with an issue, both persons must be committed to honesty. This is the only way that you can come to an agreement that both people can feel good about. I count on my wife being honest with me. It certainly might be ego inflating to have her agree with me on everything; but the real question is, would it be good for us overall? We need the honest input of each spouse.

"For *we are members of one another*. Never lose sight of the fact that we belong to each other. The two spouses make a team. The team is one, and one is the team. Be careful of outside sources that strive to enter into the mix with unbiblical like information. Often this advice starts out with, "If it were me… So, and so". When trying to help others engaged in trying to find a solution to an uncomfortable divide, my best role is to give guidance along biblical constructs. God's way is so much simpler and practical than some of the things that we come up with. We are one; and certainly as Dr. Charles Myricks stated, ***"We are better together"***.

"Be angry, and do not sin" It is interesting that the Bible does not say don't get angry. We as humans, living on this planet, subject to the things of life, will get angry from time to time. God recognizes that we will get frustrated, and angry. It is inescapable. However, God adds a proviso that commands us not to sin. In other words, we are to exercise discipline over our behavior. There is a stopping point in our anger. At that stopping point, we must begin to pull back our emotions. People who allow their anger to run amok often say things, and do things, that cross the lines of decency. Allowing one's self to get out of control usually finds the uncontrolled person going back in an effort to clean up their bad behavior. It is much easier not to go there in the first place, than to have to exercise a hasty retreat backwards, offering endless apologies.

"Do not let the sun go down on your wrath" I am laughing when I say God really wants to help some of us out. He already acknowledges that we have the capacity to get angry, and He also knows, that some of us would not let it go unless He gives us a time frame. How long can you stay angry? I've known people who have gotten angry with someone, and that anger lasted years. In fact, some have gone to the grave angry.

Recently, a pastor friend whispered in my ear that he had no idea why another pastor friend had been angry with him for years. It probably has gone on so long that the pastor who was angry does not remember the reason himself. The Bible remedy is simply, don't let the sun go down before you have settled it. Why would God take such an approach? Well, it is because He knows, the longer we carry it, the more it will increase in its intensity. Settle it early! Avoid stressful build up. God is watching!

The scripture says, *"nor give place to the devil"*. Yes, yes, yessss, the devil wants a place! He goes about to -and—fro, seeking a place. Do you recall the incident where Jesus was approaching a graveyard where a wild man lived? The wild man sought out Jesus, asking Him what He intended to do with him. Jesus saw that the man was demon possessed and spoke to the demons directly. The multiple demons began to beg Jesus not to dispel them to nothingness, but rather let them enter into a herd of pigs. (The demons needed bodies to inhabit) Jesus, knowing the outcome, allowed them to enter into the pigs, which in turn, all rushed off into the sea and drowned.

Listen, the devil dwells in many homes, and starts many fights. He is the author of confusion! Don't give him a place to live. Expel him! If he's in your home, pray him out and do not allow him to return. Exercise control over him. The Bible says, **"Resist the devil and he will flee"**!

Ephesians 4 vs. 25–27:

> *Therefore, putting away lying, "Let each one of you*
> *speak truth with his neighbor," for we are members*
> *of one another. 26 "Be angry, and do not sin": do*
> *not let the sun go down on your wrath, 27 nor give*
> *place to the devil.*

Again, we see these Ephesians scriptures as timely advice, and principles of operation. Notice that each of them pulls us closer in our relationship, not away from each other. If there is separation at all, it would be from our common enemy the devil. Only the devil would promote separation as a means of coming together. We can see his tactics working in the case of Laura and Powell. Instead of dealing truthfully with their issues they were more interested in defending their personal position. They refused to look for ways to strengthen their oneness. Laura, helped to break that oneness by angrily leaving home. After that, all kinds of suspicions and innuendos floated into their minds. All of this presented a lot of refuse that would have to be dealt with later on a deeper level. Not only would they have to deal with whatever was causing them conflicts in the first place, but now an unneeded junk collection.

FOR YOUR NOTES & REFLECTIONS

....

....

....

....

....

....

....

....

....

....

....

....

....

....

CHAPTER 5

Locking Doors

IN CHAPTER 6, I will talk a lot about going back in one's mind to recapture memories of the good things that delighted us in the past. This method certainly follows the Philippians 4:8 model by concentrating our thoughts on positive things.

For some folks, there are some trouble spots from their past that continue plaguing them into their present-day life. Our personal history should encompass things good and bad. However, if there are things to be learned from something that was not too pleasant in our past, we should learn it, and then move on! The scripture text wants us to separate out those good things and begin dwelling on those good things. It just makes so much sense to let go of the past bad stuff and hold onto the good things. It may not be quite as easy as it sounds.

Just about every couple starts out with some kind of dream. Most have long range goals or dreams that they realize they will not reach overnight. But since we cannot exactly control our future, we have to be willing to do the best we can, based on the situations handed to us. Yet in reality we have to take it like it comes and try to make lemonade when handed a bunch of lemons. I like the commercial that says, *"Life comes at you fast."* It is not wrong to have dreams and make plans. We just need to posture ourselves as the future unfolds the best we can.

So much for the future, however, every once in a while, there comes the opportunity to counsel a couple who has been wrestling with a problem from the past that won't go away. Somebody did something or said something that has erected a nasty troublesome barrier. Everything else is pretty good but this one thing just will not go away. Some people say, *"Oh just forget it and move on."* Not so easily done. Everything else is pretty good; however, it is difficult to shake this one thing!

With the Warrens it was a short affair. The Browns got into a horrible physical altercation. The Edwards blew off steam by using offensive name-calling. On and on we could go, but I think you get the point.

*I've come up with what I call, **"The Method of Locking Doors."*** Janie cannot un-slapped Glynn, and he cannot un-push her down. In order to move on, all of these couples need to learn and **practice** *the method of 'Locking Doors.'*

When a couple comes to the place of impasse and there is nothing else that can be done to erase an erratic behavior or bad event, there has to be *the striking of a covenant.* Therefore, <u>**a character binding agreement needs to be established**</u> *to hold each person to a mutual commitment.*

What I suggest is for the couple to imagine a huge door with a padlock. They must agree together to place that thing, or event, behind that imaginary door and lock it! After agreeing to place it behind the door, they must also agree to leave it there, never to return there again. They cannot go back to see how those hurdles are coming along. They've agreed to move on. Moving on is not looking back. Cut a blood covenant from now until death by leaving it there. They cannot solve it; they just can't! It is like a ravenous beast that cannot be let out into the room. We don't want to go there again; don't want to talk about it and don't want to think about it period! It will only bring the same old pain and will eat you alive. For example, I have a friend where someone cheated him out of some real estate. Every time he thinks about it; he wants to go bomb this woman's house. He needs to put this behind this door and move on. What she stole cannot be regained. She out-slicked him and the law can't touch her. Let it go, move on. A lesson has been learned, move on!

The Ortega's struggled for years blaming each other for the mutual adultery done in their marriage. They tried to discover the reasons for their unfaithfulness, such as who did what first, back and forth they went. This was a perfect opportunity for me to introduce to them **the practice of locking doors**. They certainly loved each other. The unfaithfulness was unfortunate! They genuinely were sorry for what had transpired, and that is a very important factor for healing. However, they both carried the scars of guilt and blame. It was definitely time for them **to move on.** What they needed to do was cut a blood covenant before God, promising to lock every door that would tempt them to go back and think about the past events. *"Do you trust each other now"*, was my question to them? I knew that they did. Anyone could see the love that they now shared. *"So then why would you let the devil steal your joy by repetitively bringing questions concerning the past which you cannot change?"* Once they covenanted to place, these past events behind an imaginary locked door, anyone could see their frustration's melt away. It was almost an immediate turnaround as they finished their joint prayer. **Oh, <u>we cannot leave prayer out!</u>** *God can do and will do the impossible.* Someone added to that phrase, ***"If you let Him!"***

When you've come to a pause in your journey and can't tunnel through, simply trust God. He not only can make an opening, but He can remove the entire mountain!

There's a popular TV ad that says, *"What's done in Vegas, stays in Vegas!"* **The Locked Door Principle** should have a similar slogan. *"What's placed behind this door stays behind this door; locked and buried for life"!*

Now I know that there are some people who naturally want to investigate things because they are curious to see how things are coming along. **Listen, you cannot fix this! <u>Only God can!</u>** That's why it is placed behind the locked door! The door is off limits! No more discussions; no need to think about it, certainly no, *"Well now that we have come this far, maybe we can now deal with it,"* talks. **Done means DONE! Forever DONE!**

In our most recent marriage conference when we were discussing this topic, one of the attendees questioned the wisdom of putting things away behind the closet door, causing them to risk festering and exploding. He felt that it would be better to try to solve it openly rather than hide it. I reminded him that I would never use the reference to a closet door because a closet door is never thought of as a permanent situation. A closet is in itself a temporary place and what I am proposing is a permanent condition that is never visited again. Secondly, I reminded him that the occurrence or disagreement had already been aired and declared by both husband and wife unsolvable. They tried vigorously but could not solve it. To continue bashing each other's defenses of something that could not be altered makes no sense. Lock it behind the door, throw away the key, walk away, and forget it! Done!

That was the problem with Megan's locked door. Every once in a while, she wanted to drag out the Bogeyman to see if she and George were now able to have an adult conversation. He did not want to talk about why his best man was discovered in a kissing scene with her after the rehearsal dinner. Someone told George about the kissing incident after the wedding. He was furious and wanted to punch Charles's lights out and leave Megan. Followed by weak excuses and strong arguments, they realized they could not bring it to an end that would satisfy. She wanted to explain that it was nothing on her part and Charles was actually trying to console her. How it got into a lip-lock was just not explainable. For several months they fought over this ordeal. She apologized. Charles apologized before he flew back to Denver, but it kept coming up. The only way I could help them was to have them agree to place it behind the door. Still Megan did not appreciate this method fully. Her husband broke off his long-term relationship with Charles and was willing to leave it alone. Maybe her conscience kept trying to find an alibi.

My counsel: the magic of the locked door is that it is not a temporary door where you place things that are too hot to handle right now. No, this door is for permanent hot issues whose handles and knobs need to be stripped off, making any entry impossible. You can't pull them out to examine, they just don't exist behind there anymore. Someone explained to me, when something is erased on a computer that it loses its name. The file is still there, somewhere, in the abyss but it has no identity. Thus, losing the ability to be recalled and activated.

Remember relationship faults and failures in that same light. In order to move on, kill the file. **The file is dead! Don't resurrect it!**

Emily took John back after he had cheated on her with another woman. She really did still love him and he had shown plenty of remorse over the affair. They were reunited in their loyalty but one thing stuck out. Emily kept demanding details every so often. John didn't want to talk about it. He was done! He acknowledged his unfaithfulness; he asked for forgiveness and wanted to move on.

"Did you bring that whoring hussy into our bedroom, into our bed? How could you do that John? Did she put on my undergarments, wash with my towels? What nasty sweet words did you say to her? Answer me! I hate you! Oh, how I hate you!" To this tirade, John stood silent as Emily marched back and forth and around their bedroom, pulling out drawers and throwing her lingerie at him and into the air. *"Tell me John did you tell her you loved her—do you love her? I hate you so much! How could you do this to me? I gave you my life and look what you did!"*

John continued his silence, because there was nothing he could say. He was guilty of delivering the deepest of hurts to the woman that he truly loved. He wished it could all be erased and not feel a knot in his throat as if it was choking the very life out of him. He had wronged Emily and was seriously sorry. So, this aftermath of her anger was to be expected.

"Oh God," he prayed, *"I am so sorry I messed up. Tell Em how deeply sorry I am. Help me to get through to her. I love her and lay no blame toward her. I messed up!"*

What Emily didn't think about is how dangerous it was to make him go back in his mind to dredge up old memories of Susanna. He wanted to move on and they both should! Knowing the lurid details of an affair is not going to erase what happened in the past. Yes, at first there needs to be a full disclosure. If there are tipping points that helped the causation, such as, *"I needed you to pay more attention to my work"* or *"I needed you to be home with me more"; "I wanted your support"; "You never seemed to be interested in what I liked, or thought"; "You were selfish and inattentive to my needs, etc."; "You were never romantic with me, or showed me love"; "You never seemed to be interested in my sexual needs and desires,"* these tipping points have to be discussed.

However, none of the above, or anything discussed can justify an affair. In the making of a marriage right from the altar, there is the vow of fidelity. No matter what, there is no justification! Discussing the tipping points should only help in restructuring the new journey.

If you are at a standstill in a painful matter, consider agreeing to place it behind an imaginary locked door. Again, the agreement is that once placed, there it remains under lock and key, and never to be visited again! This will surely help many couples who have had a riff in the fabric of their marriage but are struggling to recover and move on. Make a blood covenant vow and move on! The meaning of a covenant is that it is cut in blood. We have heard about the early American Indians who would cut the arms of two individuals and mingle these cut arms together in an act of unity and agreement. Out of this grew the term Blood Brothers. Marriage counselor Jimmy Evans points out that covenant far outweighs a contract. Back in early Hebrew times, a virgin's bleeding at her husband's penal penetration was so significant that her parents gathered their bloody sheets as covenantal proof of her virginity and purity. The legal bonding of their marriage was based, so to speak, on these bloody sheets.

Some will need the help of a counselor to lock their door. The counselor will provide guidance and a type of security. But the whole thing is: ***"You have got to move on!"***

Again, doors locked need to remain locked forever, or as the old saying goes, *"until Jesus comes."* After that it will make no difference anyway!

Perhaps the following form may prove helpful in structuring a locking door formula.

SOUND MARRIAGE MINISTRIES
VOLUME 3—No. 8 Dr. David Stevens
LOCKING DOORS—RESOLVING OLD
ISSUES AND MOVING ON

Often a couple cannot move beyond a certain point because of a lot of anger, hostility, and unresolved bitterness actually stemming from something so deep in the past that the actual issue, or issues have been forgotten. However, because of these issues, spouse "A" begins to resent spouse "B" and almost inevitably exhibits negative behavior that eventually causes spouse "B" to act in kind.

When there are children involved, a situation may intensify because the wounded parties are now looking for allies, thus dragging the innocent along. The spouses, while fighting their cause, are literally so absorbed that they often fail to see the damage done to their children. Sometimes other innocent people are dragged into the fray as well! (See Proverbs 22:24–25) (Philippians 4:9).

The situation is often not hopeless if we can cut through all of the surrounding refuse, to get to the actual issues that by now may be clouded and buried. So, our first step is to get the issue, or issues out in the open. To those trying to work it out, remember you can only deal with one issue at a time. This must be agreed to by both spouses.

The following formula has been used to help many warring couples resolve their issues and begin the healing process:

A. *Person "**A**" <u>must state old issue(s)</u>*

    1. *Example: "You hurt me when…"*
    2. *Example: "I felt so betrayed by you when…"*
    3. *Example: "I trusted you and you broke my heart when…"*

B. *Person "**B**" <u>must then answer the issue</u> placed on the table (Proverb 15:1, 4)*

    1. *Acknowledge the issue and the resulting hurt: "Your issue is valid and I'm sure I hurt you when…"*

    2. *"Would you forgive me based on my promise to end this behavior now?"*

    3. *"I was wrong to have caused this to become an issue. Will you accept <u>my</u> <u>apology and my promise for a different future?</u>"*

C. *Person "**B**" should now ask spouse "**A**" if they might place this past issue and the resulting hurt(s) behind an imaginary door, locking it shut with a commitment to never again revisit this door. (Philippians 4:8).*

    1. *This commitment now becomes a covenant.*

2. *This issue can never be revisited and built upon (Ephesians 4:31–32).*

3. *By covenant, you have agreed to refuse entry by mind, language, or deed.*

D. *Person "B" should now ask spouse "A" if they might place this past issue and the resulting hurt(s) behind an imaginary door, locking it shut with a commitment to never again revisit this door. (Philippians 4:8).*

1. *This commitment now becomes a covenant.*

2. *This issue can never be revisited and built upon (Ephesians 4:31–32).*

3. *By covenant, you have agreed to refuse entry by mind, language, or deed.*

4. *By covenant, you have agreed to refuse entry by mind, language, or deed.*

Party A .... *Date* ....
Party B .... *Date* ....

May the <u>HOLY SPIRIT OF GOD</u> witness this agreement in honor of the Word.

FOR YOUR NOTES & REFLECTIONS

Christ Center Church of God
1615 W. Chelten Avenue

....

....

....

....

....

....

....

....

....

....

....

....

....

....

CHAPTER 6

Oh No! Cold Showers Again???

BESIDES THIS CURRENT title: OH NO, COLD SHOWERS AGAIN??? I wrestled with some other thoughts for a fitting title such as: WHY AM I IN THIS COLD SHOWER or THIS COLD WATER IS NOT HELPING ME ONE BIT, or WHY DO I HAVE TO BE HORNY ALONE, and finally WHY AM I CHOSEN to be FROZEN, but I think you have the idea of what this chapter is about.

Someone asked this question, *"Pastor—if your wife or husband does not want to have sex as often as you, what should a spouse do? Is that grounds for separation or should you grin and bear it and take a cold shower???"*

Thanks Dana from Facebook by asking an excellent question concerning the difference of sexual desire displayed between husband and wife. Marriage should be based on love. Love demands cooperation, compromise, sacrifice, and contentment. It is not unusual for some spouses to have different sexual desires when it comes to how much and how often. If one spouse is highly charged and the other is on low voltage, they have to work toward a middle ground. They both have to cooperate and sacrifice some. Spouse A may want an everyday event and spouse B once a week. Having sex every day will not satisfy Spouse B just like having it once a week will not satisfy Spouse A. Perhaps they can settle on something like 3 days, spread out during the week. The Bible says that the husband's body belongs to his wife and her body belongs to him. If she loves him as she should, then his needs are important to her. If he loves her, he should find ways to put her needs ahead of his own. This is mature love. Selfish love never works for harmony. So, in the interest of harmony, Spouse A has given into moving away from demanding the 7 days of sex for an intimate 3 days with Spouse B. Then Spouse B in the interest of harmony, has to tack on 2 more days than originally desired. Also, both spouses need to know not to hold each other to a too strict accounting. Harmony will bring on variance from time to time. It is OK in the name of love. Marriage again calls for cooperation, compromise (storge'), sacrifice (agape'), and contentment (phile'o). Love is always giving and never about being selfish!

I am almost certain that cold showers don't work; unless you can figure out how to get that cold water into the mind where sex begins.

In my book Marriage: Catching A Second Wind, there is a chapter called SEX MATTERS. I plan to take some excerpts from it in this chapter which shares details on putting some romantic spice back into the relationship. Some of that spice is sexual. I hear all the time, people making excuses like, they are too tired once they get off from work; too engaged in other activities; getting older; having other priorities; too old for it to matter; etc. May I offer the most astute, well thought out reactionary comment to the entire above notion:

HOGWASH!

Check out Genesis 2:24 and Matthew 19:5, where the Bible is giving the basic foundation for marriage. No one has the right to arbitrarily exclude intimacy from this foundational principle.

Let me now share some excerpts from my book, Marriage: Catching A Second Wind, Chapter 6 **Sex Matters:

**   The reader will benefit more by reading the entire chapter 6, entitled "Sex Matters" found in Dr. David Stevens' book **Marriage: Catching A Second Wind** obtained from www.soundmarriages.

Gerard and his wife have not been sexually intimate for over a decade. Interestingly, just like they don't deal with each other sexually, they don't deal with each other in any other areas either. Kelly and Sam have gone almost 15 years without having intercourse after the birth of their third daughter. Their relationship is about as bad as it can get. While Gerard and Diane ignore each other, Kelly and Sam choose to yell violently at each other all the time. Then there is the example of Patricia and Charles who engage in sex maybe every three or four months, providing that they are not mad with each other at the time. We need to be careful to recognize that every marriage where sexual intimacy is not being regularly practiced is not necessarily one where they are sniping at each other. For a while they may get along, but watch out, don't take it lightly. This kind of behavior is certain to be a love killer.

Rarely, if ever, do you find couples that avoid each other sexually, in a great love place. When intimacy is missing over an extended period of time, they will not tell you honestly that they are happy in love. No sex at this point usually represents an ugly impasse that will lead to certain destruction in the relationship. Remember these couples probably did not plan this separation at first but it gets easier and easier down the road. There are some marriages managing to go along on an empty love tank, without bitterness at first, but trust me the storm

Com; www.Amazon.com or www.barnesandnobles.com or email or call Christ Center: ccenter22cog@gmail.com 215-548-7483.

is coming. There are usually two noted responses to a missing pattern of sexual intimacy. It will show up as cool indifference or volatile rage.

Ernest and Joan tend to ignore each other with a cool indifference. They would explain it as being too old to care about that part of their lives. That's an interesting excuse, but why the noted indifference toward each other? Then what about that statement: we are too old to care? Is there any age limit?

Actually, if we trust biblical mandate, we find that sex involves one third of the covenantal marriage makeup and it does not say anything about an age limit. If you look at the history of Abraham and Sarah, how was she able to give birth at age 90? The age was amazing, of course, but this means they must have been having sex all along. Sexual intercourse wasn't only to produce children but as a natural marital relationship practice.

Oh, and just for the record, did you know that after Sarah died at the age of 127, Abraham was then around 137, and he got married again? That's right he married Katurah, and they had 6 children over a period of 38 years. Not too shabby old Abe; therefore, I'm smiling for you! (Several noted Jewish historians have concluded from their research that Hagar and Katurah were one and the same.)

I have been teaching for many years what I call, The Triangular Plan, based on the writings of Walter Trobish. This plan is also found in Genesis, the first book of Bible, chapter

2, verse 24. The scriptural formula divides marriage into three specific sections or actions. It mentions **Leaving**, as the public lawful separation from parents and others as a first step. Next it instructs that **Cleaving** is the vowing of an emotional and/ or physical commitment to love and fidelity. Then there is that interesting term, **"One flesh"** that finalizes the covenant. One flesh is the exclusive spiritual, physical, and mental relational factor shared with married partners. It takes these three elements to have a legitimate consummated marriage.

I suggest looking at the Gen.2:24 passage which is where I derive my illustration of a three-legged stool that sets the whole foundation of a marriage. In order for the stool to stand, it must have each of its legs planted squarely on the ground. If a leg is removed, the stool will fall on the ground. I am certainly not trying to make any of the legs more important than any of the others. They are all important. Yet they must all be there in order to do the job as it was intended.

I am pretty convinced that in a great many of the cases I have observed over the years where there is long-term marital conflict, sexual intimacy is either completely missing or it is practiced so slightly that it might as well be missing. I can understand why people in a troubled marital condition don't feel like being intimate. Even if they were having it physically, it certainly is not going to be in any way intimate. True intimacy taps into the mental, emotional, and spiritual, as well as the physical.

It is a well-known fact that anger will steal the joy from intimacy.

Yet on the other hand I believe that there are many married couples who are not particularly upset with each other but have carelessly adopted a no sex—or little sex mentality!

Warning: this usually will become cool indifference which is another form of rage. Whether volatile or cool, the results are the same. They both are love killers.

If sex is to be clearly understood from the Genesis 2:24 passage, then its' place of importance is one third of the marriage equation. Just as the other two tenets of the marriage triangle need to be regularly practiced, the one flesh relationship that Dr. Tim LaHaye calls "The Marriage Act," must also be regularly practiced. There are all kinds of theories about how many times, and how often is normal sexual activity? If there was a "Normal," it would set the bar for everyone to follow. What might be even "Normal" for a couple in their first 10 years may increase or decrease in their next 10 years. Who can predict?

So, setting an average normal number of times a couple should have intercourse is not possible, because people are varied individuals. Each couple has their own unique chemistry. I can imagine if we could give a factual number of times that sexual intercourse should be practiced. It would only provide another point for specific groups of analysts to fight over.

No actually, the bar is set by a married couple's private decisions. It is up to them exclusively, as long as it does not fall into the realm of being ridiculous. Ridiculous (ruling out illness, etc.) is for a married couple living in the same space to go weeks and months at a time without engaging in the Marriage Act.

Again, we can agree upfront that if they live in different cities because of work, etc., and can only get together when time and distance permits, this does not count as an intentional violation. Any situations of an unusual nature are excluded from this conversation. The funny thing here is that these are not the people having the problems of inconsistency. They seem to have no problem working it out. I once heard the story of a famous jet-set couple who lived on two different coasts. They said, *"We plan our get-togethers as being great celebrations. When we get together it is always shooting stars and Roman candles."*

Sex definitely does matter in the marital life of the contented. In God's design, sexual intimacy helps to bring about contentment. Just as we have pointed out in the book Marriage: The Rules of the Game, 'sex is not love, and love is not sex,' but they do act to support each other.

My concern for sexual intimacy is directed more toward a couple's pattern regularity. This is not based so much on the number of times, but more on the regularity or irregularity. We understand that things happen. This may alter times, but if we look more at the pattern of things it would give a better picture of the couples' intimate health. Again, we take a look at what the Marriage Makers' book says on the subject.

1. Corinthians 7:5 says, *"Do not deprive one another except with consent <u>for a time</u> that you may give yourselves to fasting and prayer; and come together again so that Satan does not tempt you because of your lack of self-control."* Notice the key phrases that stick out:

1. *Do not deprive* (sexually)
2. *Except with consent*
3. *For a time*
4. (for) *prayer and fasting*
5. (in order to) come together again (sexually)
6. (*so* that) *Satan does not tempt you* (*while you are not being intimate with each other*).

The scripture is pointing out clearly that when we are fasting, we are not to engage in sexual experiences of any kind.

However, let's not forget the strong scriptural implication here, is that *there should be an agreement* before entering into a period of fasting as well as a reasonable time limit. A husband or a wife should not decide independently one day, *"I'm going to fast."* Nor should they set a long-term date that is unreasonable. There has to be an agreement that is practical and beneficial. The Marriage Maker's book says that his body belongs to her, and her body belongs to him. There can't be an, *"Oh baby, didn't I tell you I'll be fasting for the next 60 days?"* you would be working against scripture. Remember in that scripture it tells us to make it brief (see v.5 *"for a time"*). Now I know that the more holy among us are going to differ with me because fasting is a very spiritual thing that is God-honoring. How dare I suggest that intimacy takes precedence over fasting? I'm sorry, but let the word speak for itself. Read again carefully 1 Corinthians 7:5 for yourself:

V.5 *Do not deprive one another except with consent for a time that you may give yourselves to fasting and prayer; and come together again so that Satan does not tempt you because of your lack of self-control.*

Then read verse 3 and 4 to gain the context:

3Let the husband render to his wife the affection due her, and likewise also the wife to her husband. 4The wife does not have authority over her own body, but the husband does. And likewise, the husband does not have authority over his own body, but the wife does. *I rest my case!*

There is that occasional time when a spouse just may not be able to perform. This is to be expected in the life of human beings. My concern centers on the normal times when a couple could be and should be intimate. The point is if you are married to each other you cannot arbitrarily decide not to be intimate with each other. Causing an argument to avoid being sexually intimate, as is practiced by some, is sin also.

Once again, to make the point from another angle, to do these rebellious acts to avoid expressing intimacy is sin, according to the Marriage Manual!

We need to spend some time talking to those who do have some genuine sexual challenges. What if you are unable to function in this area of your marriage? First, we need to affirm that there is no sin here. If there is a problem of physical discomfort, we are fortunate to be living in times of great medical enlightenment. I believe that God has invested a great amount of ever-increasing knowledge into the mind banks of medical practitioners. I also believe that if you are facing sexual challenges that there are expert physicians out there who can help you. Don't you and your spouse suffer in silence?

Please do not give up. Help can be on the way. If God has given us this beautiful gift, it is unlikely that He would not supply the answer to our problems. Yet it is incumbent upon us to do everything in our power to find a cure. Don't give up, don't give in. Seek diligently for God's way! If God has given us the incredible gift of sexual intimacy, He must have a way for us to fulfill that gift. It starts with prayer!

I know a lot of religious people don't understand it, or believe it, but sex was placed there by God, and placed there for a reason. God planned it that way from the beginning. **Ignore it and it has the power to destroy a marital relationship.** Work with it and it has the power to bring health, healing, and contentment. It keeps the flow going in the marital relationship.

When I urged Jameson and Amy to make sexual intimacy a regular part of their relationship, they began to see a new level of harmony sprouting. Sex took the edge off of their marriage issues. Arguments began to lessen and practically disappear. Once the enjoyment of totally loving each other caught on, they seemed not to be able to keep their hands off of each other. After they followed this advice, I didn't want to call them, and certainly did not want to visit them, because it was likely that they were spending a lot of private time, doing who knows what; smile! They went from zero to full tilt, on this one!

FOR YOUR NOTES & REFLECTIONS

Christ Center Church of God
1615 W. Chelten Avenue

....

....

....

....

....

....

....

....

....

....

....

....

....

....

CHAPTER 7

Memories Old and New

MY FRIEND ROCHELLE asked, *"Can a married spouse fall out of love, and if so, was it real love in the first place?"* My answer was, *"Yes and yes!"*

Andre Crouch wrote a gospel song; Take Me Back Where I First Believed. Sometimes couples whose love has grown cold need to take the time to go back to where they first believed. In the beginning there was something there that drew them into a love relationship. I know this personally because it is etched in my mind. The first time I saw my wife to be, I was stopped dead in my tracks, like never before, and from there ever after!

MY STORY:

Every year at the end of the college semester I was packed and on the way home, as soon as you could say three words, *"Finals are over!"* When that last final was finished, I automatically said, *"Philadelphia here I come!"*

It was a real mystery to me why I could not get it together that one year to go home. For some reason I felt that I needed to stay in Indiana that summer. I really was not looking forward to being in that Indiana heat at all. But there was that nagging feeling that I needed to plant my feet there at this time. I had to figure out how I was going to make it financially and where I was going to live for the summer. While sorting it all out, Jim, a student from Africa, came to me with a proposal to manage his construction job for a month. He had to take a trip somewhere and needed someone to hold down his spot. It was ideal since I was about to look for work.

The boss agreed to the switch and I was hired. Construction work is no joke! I handled the mud mixing detail. I had to supply three or four brick layers working on the second floor while still building up. This was an interesting job because after mixing the concrete I then had to deliver it to them by shoveling it upward in a backward motion, and then slamming the mixture neatly onto some concrete platforms. After losing several loads, I finally got it pretty close to accurate, but I'm telling you it was not easy in that Indiana sun.

At the beginning of the third week after I had gotten used to this type of hard work, Jim returned earlier than we had agreed on. He and Big Jim Withers, the boss, came over to me. While I was in the middle of mixing concrete, Big Jim (that's what everyone called him) announced that although he was satisfied with my work, little Jim had the job first, and he just could not afford to have us both working. I had to hand in my safety helmet and shovel on the spot. Talk about being unfair.

Remember, I was away from home, and school was over. I was on my own, and I had to find a job quickly. So, I went to the local unemployment agency, but they had nothing except there was someone who needed a painter for a small private job. Well, that was something I could do. *"I'll take it,"* I told the interviewer.

My parents taught me how to paint growing up, and I got to be very good at it. I took the job and found myself in business. One satisfied customer's reference led to another painting job, and so I was in business, and the business was growing.

I had a college friend named Ray, and rumor had it that his fiancée and his sister were coming to visit him for a week or so. For some reason I got real excited to meet his sister. I was so excited that I decided after work to stop by his apartment still in my painter clothes. This was very unusual and different for me. You've got to know I always loved dressing up. Even then as a poor college student with very little money, I wanted to look dapper.

It was kind of a Philadelphia thing that caused me to grow up liking cool looking clothes. I worked during my high school years in a neighborhood department store where I learned that many of the fashionable salesmen went to Harry's, a small downtown wholesale haberdashery. Harry's sold to salespeople at bargain prices. So, Harry's was the place for me. I've always liked matching outfits; everything had to be just right. Even when I was dressing down, I wanted a certain look. This practice remains to this day. I like to match when I'm just planning to wear Jeans and a T shirt. It is a Philadelphia thing like I said.

On this occasion however, there was no time to do all of that. I knew that there was an announced plan for Ray and Betty to go out on a double date that evening with his sister and another friend named George. Going home to shower and change would delay, or even prevent meeting his sister until the next day. So, unlike my normal pattern, I decided that the time I had was now. Tomorrow could be another story! I parked my car and went straight for his door, painter duds and all.

I walked into Ray's pad (that's what we called an apartment back then) and there she was! Dorothy sat there in a black and white checkered jacket with a black straight skirt. Beautiful, beautiful! Sparkling eyes, long hair, great legs, and gorgeous skin; she had it all! When she opened her perfect mouth out came this deep, smooth, sophisticated voice that drew me fully in. I was almost speechless, certainly stunned.

Inside of my brain the circuits were misfiring with all kinds of jumbled information. Right there I knew I had been struck by Cupid's love-laden arrows. The whole quiver I might add. Yes, I was in love! I wanted to marry her! Wow, was she free; was there anyone else in the picture? I didn't care! I wanted her!

Sadly, after spending some wonderful time with her, I realized the time was approaching for that dreaded prearranged double date. I hated it but what could I do? I couldn't tell them, *"Hold up, I'm in love with your sister and this date you have is interfering with my love life."* Ray and his fiancée Betty, Dorothy and his friend George, who they were waiting to arrive, were very near to leaving, so I excused myself and went next door to my apartment. I showered and dressed quickly, hoping to get a glimpse of her again before they left. When I got back outside, the four of them were already in the car and pulling out from the curb. I just barely got a glimpse of her sitting in the backseat looking back at me standing there. What a sad moment. I was sure that this would be the only separation of this kind in our future. She was surely the answer to my romantic dreams and my prayers.

DOROTHY'S STORY:

I had been teaching in the Charleston South Carolina school district and was on my summer break. I wasn't sure what I was going to do for the summer. My friend Betty and I talked about going to Florida for a vacation. Then my brother

Raymond, who was engaged to Betty, invited us to come to Anderson Indiana, where he went to school. He wanted us to stay there for a couple of weeks. So, we decided that the Indiana trip would be our best choice since neither of us had ever been there before.

Our visit was during the time the Church of God held its annual camp meeting. There were crowds of people present from all over the country and even abroad. We went to the morning service in this big dome auditorium. I loved it! The choir, the speaker, even the audience seemed full of enthusiasm so this experience was quite different from my small congregation in Charleston, South Carolina.

That afternoon Ray registered Betty and me at a local hotel and then brought us back to his apartment. While sitting there, many of his friends came in to visit. Ray had told his friends that his sister and his fiancée were coming to town and that he wanted them to meet us. This one fine looking guy came in and I said to myself, *"Gee, it would be so nice if he would come over and speak to me."* Well he did and we had a great conversation but much too short for my liking. Ray had arranged for Betty and his friend George and me to go out on a dinner date that evening. David, this new guy, said he had to go home just before we were to leave for this dinner date. I was feeling kind of sad that he did not go with us to town to the local Frisch's Big Boy Restaurant, but the four of us going out together had been previously arranged. I remembered seeing

David again briefly as we all piled into Ray's small car. I saw David standing on the curb looking our way as the car slowly pulled away. He was so fine! He had changed his clothes. Wow! I couldn't help wishing that he was the one taking me out to eat.

Later I learned that David ran from there across campus to tell his friend Richard, whom I had met many years before at the West Middlesex camp meeting in Pennsylvania, that he just met his wife! Richard told him that I was an old friend. The next day David and I met and he asked me to go to a concert with him. I enjoyed the concert so much and being with him was so nice. The next day he asked me to go to town with him, things in my head and heart were moving so fast. I didn't want to run him away. So, I declined to go, thinking maybe it would help to slow things down; I'm not sure why I did this to this day. Betty asked me if I was crazy and did, I want to lose him? I didn't but I thought we should slow things down a bit even though we had not even hugged at that point. She thought that was a really crazy idea. I did too afterwards. I just did not want to seem too anxious and have him lose interest.

I learned that David was kind of short on money so things had to be measured out. One great date did not cost any money. He took us to see a drive-in outdoor movie. The catch was we drove to the rear of the outdoor theater where you could see the picture on the screen but could not hear the sound. At one point strangely enough, we were suddenly surrounded by what looked like millions of fireflies (or some call them lightning bugs). That was a wonderful evening; just sitting there in his cool looking sports car and watching a movie without sound, with millions of fireflies dancing around us. David and I had so much fun even without the sound. I found that he was a gentleman and I appreciated that so much. As a finale, he asked me if I would mind if he kissed me. By this time, I was more than ready. We were in love!

Before I left Indiana, he proposed and I accepted. Betty went back to Charleston, but I went to visit my aunt in Pennsylvania. We were in love and planned to get married! My aunt and uncle were so surprised but delighted at the news that I had met someone and was planning to get married to him. Later that summer David joined us in Sharon, Pennsylvania. My folks fell in love with him and I had their approval. He then took me to meet his parents in Philadelphia. It was official; **we were in love and planned to get married! Woo hoo!**

OUR HISTORY TOGETHER:

Well now, that was over 60 years ago and as you can see those memories are still very vivid in our minds. This is an example of what I am referring to when I say, *"Return in your mind to when you first fell in love."* Even now, those memories can give me goose pimples. That first kiss was like violins playing, fireworks launching, and strawberries dancing on our tongues. **Excuse me, I may need to take a little praise**

break right about here and do a little victory dance after writing this, smile!

Good memories can help heal fresh wounds! Couples in trouble often are in trouble because they are dwelling too much in the present moments. I am very much a realist, however if you are in a bad place right now, treat it as a momentary thing; it can get better. Notice that I said *it can get better*. **It all depends on you.** Either these rough things will get better or maybe not. It is all up to you. I prefer to look at these situations with hope. I believe life will get better because that's what I'm looking for it to do. The Clarke Sisters sing the song, *"I'm looking for a miracle—I expect the impossible..."* That's what I'm talking about! Looking for and expecting good to triumph over everything else. Again Philippians 4:9 says to concentrate on the positive stuff which will crowd out the negative.

REALITY CHECK and a TV Drama:

OK, on the practical side, you or your spouse may have messed up but **is it worth flushing a lifetime over a mistake?**

On the popular TV show Grey's Anatomy Christina's husband was foolishly willing to throw his whole marriage into jeopardy because she was not ready to give him a child. I do understand that it was important to him, but there was still time, age wise. *They should've had an understanding before they got married about when-and-if.* **When and if to have children should not have come as a surprise.** I think that she was refusing because of her emerging career as a surgeon. I missed several episodes but it seems that during their feud he broke their fidelity because he was angry, frustrated, and disappointed. He had sex with someone just to have sex. Later, he wanted Christina to reconsider letting him back into her heart. He said his indiscretion was just sex, no love, just sex!

Listen Owen, if you wanted Christina to have your child what did *"just sex"* outside of your marriage have to do with that desire? From the scope of it, it would seem that you were claiming it was just sex, meaning you were not trying to impregnate during your adultery. So, I'm confused at just what you were attempting to do. Perhaps you were confused about what you were attempting to do. I know that this is TV but I also see it as reality because many people in real life make the same kind of foolish decisions based on *"just sex."* In the TV reality, his wife refused to give him a child. I do understand again the seriousness that he felt. However, he messed up his relationship by acting like a little kid on the playground who says, *"If you won't let me play the way I want to play -I'm taking my basketball home."* Analyzing the situation, I would say he made a desperate immature move that would naturally lead to a crippling disaster. However, after having said all of that in real life their marriage could have been saved. But for starters both of them would have to start acting like adults, **getting past the past, and learning to embrace the principles of good decision-making.**

Yes, it was bad on his part. Perhaps just as bad on her part. But if this were in real life, they would have promised to have a marriage based on loving each other in sickness, and in health, and all the other promises made at an altar. I have seen real life marriages where the same or similar bad judgments have side-tracked and almost utterly destroyed a marriage relationship but hope prevailed. The will and the desire to hang onto their marriage, and the dream they started together won out overall.

I am not sure where the TV relationship of a Christina and Owen would take us, TV being TV, but **I do know in real God driven lives, that exercising the principles of forgiveness, trust, and faith in God and His profound Word, will help a couple overcome!**

FOR YOUR NOTES & REFLECTIONS

....

....

....

....

....

....

....

....

....

....

....

....

....

....

CHAPTER 8

Kindness Kounts

Trust me I do know how to spell *"counts"* with a *"C"*. **Spelling it with a *"K"* was to gain your full attention!** Have you ever noticed in some marriage relationships, where there is a lack of kindness displayed by one or both of the partners? In the life practices of this couple, we would notice a general pattern of non-kindness. It may however be something that they are willing to overlook, but I think that kindness is always in style. There is never a time when a spouse can be cruel, uncaring, and unthinking toward the other spouse. This should be true even in times when they are not feeling pleasant toward each other. Somewhere I remember saying in something I wrote about myself; *"I am a winner and because*

I am a winner, I think in terms of winning by utilizing the best methods of winning." What I mean by this, even if I'm at odds I don't want to destroy the possibility of a good relationship because of using destructive forces. I may not agree with you, but in disagreeing, I don't need to try to tear you down, and make you feel less of a person. When all is said and done, at the end of an argument, the opponent should still feel a sense of genuine respect directed towards them. Not really so focused on the importance of winning or losing but looking at the positive maintenance of the relationship. This principle of operation should hold true whether there is a disagreement with a coworker, relative, friend, opponent, and certainly a spouse. Even one's enemies should go away from a dispute feeling that they have not been deliberately set upon, and disgraced.

I believe in the 1936 Dale Carnegie philosophy of How to Win Friends and Influence People. Better than that, I recall the word of God saying that *'love is kind, and patient, gentle, and long-suffering.'* Even in an argument it is good for the opponents to feel that they can carry something positive away from the experience.

Zara and Sam are not in a good place these days because their Kindness aptitude is strained. Well it is like this: Zara just does not seem to be into her husband. Sam is a loving, giving man with a heart full of love. He is attentive to his wife, often going out of his way to do things to please her. He never forgets her birthday, their anniversary, Christmas, Valentine's

Day, etc., and all the days in between. The problem here is that the attention to giving and sharing is not reciprocal. Zara goes about life as though she could care less. She is almost never encouraging, ignores celebration times, and gives very little affection. At first Sam because of his natural enthusiasm did not notice. After a while, it began to get through to him that what he was putting out, was in no favorable measure being returned. I saw him with tears in his eyes one day after a major giving holiday. He had gone all out to buy her a special ring that he had to make a great sacrifice to buy. She did remember the occasion this time by purchasing him an umbrella. So, you probably are thinking, "Well it must have been a money issue." No, actually Zara makes quite a bit more than her husband, and he pays most of the major bills. So, it is not finance but intent that we are looking at. Zara's lack of kindness, noted as carelessness which is beginning to sow seeds of bitterness in Sam's heart.

OK Mr. Counselor, what is the cure here? Well, this is a serious problem. My counsel to Sam is that he begin by really seeking for an answer from God. There are some issues that no matter our intentions, or abilities, we just cannot solve. Sam's first solution was to ignore her idiosyncrasies and pretend that they did not exist. Probably after that he felt that showering her with abundant affection would cause her to reciprocate. Then the anger and frustration drove him to arguments and complaints. All of the above failed. Even counseling to a large degree did little good. You see, there are some things that are buried so deeply that only God can get to them. Sam must begin with concentrated prayer to God for divine guidance and intervention. God can, and we can't!

Because Zara does not seem to have a clue, I do think counseling is needed also. This couple should sit down with a counselor who can help them place their differences on the table to see where their relationship stands. Pretending that all is well while at least one of them is suffering is not going to be beneficial to either. Sometimes in life people do things to save face, but underneath there is a boiling cesspool. This is where Sam's issues are headed. It is better to bring things out in the open to be assessed and evaluated. What can be seen can be fixed more readily than that which is covered up. Often in the Christian community we feel that by not acknowledging wrongdoing it will disappear. This is not likely to happen. What is more likely to happen here is that those buried things that are brewing beneath the surface, one day will boil over with uncontrollable power. The thing that is squashed and ignored while brewing will become stronger. At some point, emotional reality will no longer be denied. It will seek its unveiling. Most often, it will result in an uncomfortable explosion of words and attitudes that are unbecoming to the mild Christian manner of which we are supposed to display. Anger, especially anger that has been seething, picks up power. Because of neglecting a proper, earlier outlet, built up anger usually throws aside all formality, manners, and decorum. Words are exchanged and insulting things said. Often name-calling and certainly blaming accompanies these angry outbursts.

Before reaching this explosive point, Sam needs to come admittedly to Zara, *"I confess I have a problem. We need help!"* The very next thing is to ask Zara to join him in a season of individual prayers for their relationship. Perhaps he could suggest one or two days, but definitely accompanied by fasting. I strongly suggest fasting because it is evident that this, above all else, is a spiritual problem. While setting this agreement up, set a time after the fast for a one on one discussion. Before reaching this explosive point, Sam needs to come admittedly to Zara, *"I confess I have a problem. We need help!"* The very next thing is to ask Zara to join him in a season of individual prayers for their relationship. Perhaps he could suggest one or two days, accompanied by fasting if possible. I strongly suggest fasting because it is evident that this, above all else, is a spiritual problem. While setting it up, set a date after they have fasted for a one on one discussion. Sam should put the emphasis on them praying for God's leading and healing.

This is extremely important, write down for the counselor what the actual issues are. It is very likely that Zara has some unresolved issues with Sam too. The worst thing would be to end up unloading on Zara in front of a counselor without her knowing previously what Sam's issues are, and the issues she is seeking help with. Jesus is very specific in both scriptures found in Matthew 17:18–21 and Mark 9:28–29 that there is an evil spirit (demon) in the mix, and that **prayer and fasting are needed to dislodge it** from its holdings.

Sometimes we allow our human nature to convince us that something is no big deal, and if we just wait long enough then it will disappear. On the contrary my friend, it only takes a spark to get a fire going. Two cautions:

1. Do not dismiss the little things that are important and should be settled early on. *In all thy getting—get understanding!*
2. Do not underestimate demonic attempts at finding footholds that cause marital stress. Our enemy, the devil, never sleeps or slumbers while seeking occasions to bring disharmony. Once these footholds have been established, it may take prayer and fasting to settle the account.

What does it take for Zara to be loving and kind to Sam? It really takes an act of the will. Loving his wife as he does, he has every right to expect her to love him in that same way. What is expected here is for them both to express agape love. We have said before that's how God loves us. **God loves us because He loves us!** That's just the way it is. He chooses to love us! God refuses to not love us! In fact, there is nothing that we can do that will cause Him to not love us. His love for us is not based on an actual reciprocal relationship. In other words, we don't have to do something to make Him love us. **God loves us first. He loves us because He chooses to love us.** It is difficult to duplicate this type of love in our marital relationship, but it is the goal that we should aim for. I should love my wife because I choose to love her, not because of something that she did, or is doing for me. That kind of action would be reciprocal love and not genuine Agape'. However, think about it, in reality, pouring out love on a spouse and getting no love in return is not all that easy to continue either. Unfortunately, this often leads to marital breakdown, separation, and divorce.

Kindness, on the other-hand, can be alluring and magnetic. It is like that state of gratefulness that makes one long to return a kindness. It reminds me of this example, in our personal life. For over a year now we have been drinking barley shakes for our added vitamin health. My wife, Dorothy gets up every morning, even in the winter time, braves the cold to make it to the kitchen, and brings me these wonderful green shakes and graham crackers. This is not something that I require her to do, but she feels that it is necessary for added well-being and does not mind braving it through the chilly house tempera-tures to enhance our health. If you asked her why, I'm sure she would say, *"Because I love him, and this is something good for his health."* When I think about this wonderful woman getting out of her warm bed to care extra for me, I certainly have no problem serving her. One small example would be that, she does not drive, so it certainly is no problem for me to drive her wherever she wants to go. We are kind to each other like that. It is a part of our love for each other. **We are grateful for each other!**

We have made it a regular part of our lives to say thank you. Each meal that she prepares I say, *"thank you."* We are often out and about these days so, I will treat us to meals, and each time she thanks me. I believe we enjoy being kind to each other.

These types of decisions are worked out in one's inner will. I like to describe this in my teaching sessions as having a bunch of large offices. Right smack in the middle there is a tiny little office with no staff. This is the will. It is surrounded by many large, fully staffed offices. Picture one of those offices as Love. It has at its command all kinds of subordinates, like emotion, passion, romance, etc. Or consider a neighboring office named Commitment. Commitment might have at its command, things like, understanding, trust, valor, duty, etc., but right in the middle is this little office called *"Will."* The work of the other offices cannot come into function until **the Will** *gives the go ahead*! **Your will makes the choice!**

I talked to someone once, who had made up their mind that they needed to divorce their mate. When I asked about the reasons for this decision, there were very few negative responses. There had been no cheating, no abuse, and no defection. It came down to that person declaring, *"I just don't want to be married to that person anymore."* I watched as friends tried to make a persuasive case for this person to reconsider leaving the marriage. But it was the will that reinserted itself. *"I just don't want to be married anymore!"*

So, even kindness is a choice. It has to go through the office of The Will. A couple that wishes to develop their union into a loving, cooperative, kind relationship must start off in that little office called The Will. *"I will be kind to you!"* This largely, is an individual decision; however, it certainly is more palatable when it is reciprocal. If I am kind to you, you certainly will feel better about being kind to me. **Kindness Kounts!**

FOR YOUR NOTES & REFLECTIONS

....

....

....

....

....

....

....

....

....

....

....

....

....

....

CHAPTER 9

So How Is Your Sex Life for Real?

BE HONEST WITH the following question. Which of the following terms best describes your marital sex life?

Hot and Steamy

Great

Good

Fair

Not too good

Poor

Bad

Worst

Missing

The list above is important in a marriage relationship. I had a conversation with someone recently, who probably would score in the fair to not too good range. It was very hard for them to determine how their marriage relationship got that way. Was it because of their spouses' non-interests in having sexual intercourse or because of their own lack of interest? Or was it just a mutual settlement for what has become the new normal for them?

Since I had some previous conversations on the subject with this person, I didn't feel that it was always about a low sex drive on the part of either spouse. No, I rather believe that because these folks are a part of a new emerging movers and shakers modality, they have allowed life to press them into this new settling type of behavior. Quietly settling with no fuss, no fanfare, they started to develop a mutual let's put this thing off for now attitude. The plan was to put off dealing with it until at least there was some time to figure it out. That's the problem, time. Sometimes we just have to stop the presses and take care of business.

Were they always there at this place? No, I don't think so. Too many late business meetings, taxiing the children to and fro, moonlighting to bring in extra finances, etc., has worn them down. This can happen gradually without couples even realizing it. We just jump in and do what is needed without thinking. Sexual intimacy becomes last on the list, and that's the real problem!

Like my dad's reference to putting oil in the car; just like the physical, spiritual, mental, and sexual healing puts oil in the relationship. Without it activated in the relationship, the relationship will cease up like a frozen engine without oil.

The societal demands on your family time will sneak up gradually, if allowed. If we do not take charge, it will develop a life of its own. The Bible says, *"It takes time to be holy."* We can build on that: it takes time to *be wholly also*. It does not happen on its own. If you do not take charge and control your time, then your time will control you.

One of the major factors that helps to take control from us is guilt. Most of us want to be perceived as nice people. When something comes up that demands our time, even if we don't have the time, we squeeze it in.

Guilt, will often push us into taking on more than we can afford to do. For example, I've noticed one of the things my wife is getting better at these days is in saying no to things that will stretch her. Listen, she is one busy First Lady of our urban church; a homemaker; grand mom; and a whole lot more. It is so easy to get caught up. Periodically, she will get a call from one of the national volunteer agencies to help run a fundraising drive. Their pitch for her is to only go to the houses on our street, door-to-door to get pledges and then to send follow-up letters to those same people. Ultimately, the callers always make it sound like it will only take a little of her time to help out a national charity. She is no longer fooled into having a guilt trip for turning them down. She does not really have the time, not to mention the extra energy it takes. What sounds like only a little extra time given could actually be the straw that breaks the camel's back. I am so proud of her; she has learned to say, *"No."* Therefore, we must learn to prioritize our daily routine.

Many things are very important in life but not very important in our personal life. We get to choose and set boundaries. In your life you have to know when to say, *"NO!"* **No, so that you can say, "YES"** to what is important! A healthy sex life is important! Sanctify the time, the space, and the place!

Once again there are 3 things stated in Genesis 2:24 that makeup the basic marriage package. These 3 things are *leaving* (the lawful public sanctioning), *cleaving* (the commitment to love and fidelity) and *one flesh* (sexual intimacy). All 3 are needed and must be working in the relationship. There is no mention of volunteerism, or any other thing that may interfere with a couple's intimate times. If you want to take marriage seriously, you have to take the instructions seriously.

The other side of it is that many of these sexless situations end with couples disliking and sometimes going as far as deeply hating each other. They did not begin that way, but with one leg of a three—legged stool missing. It becomes increasingly hard to keep that stool balanced over a long period of time.

When I was a young child, I learned to ride my tricycle on two wheels. I could go for long runs that way but eventually I had to bring it down to its third wheel. That's how it was designed to operate in spite of my daring and ingenuity. Marriage was intended to function on three principles. The triangular plan was designed by God to function with these three elements working together. Certainly, in a case where a partner cannot perform in special instances like illness, location, temporary stress, etc., there can be an understanding and cooperation to fulfill the sexual intimacy gap. That's part of love and commitment, and reasonable common sense.

I've had conversations with so many couples who've just allowed their intimate life to drift away. Some of them don't even have a clue when and how it all began. Another long meeting, or being too exhausted, and their ship began to slowly sink. There was never any intention to allow their relationship to fall into a deep loveless pit. But carelessness also has its negative rewards.

I believe emphatically that the church must teach this to Christians. Most of the world outside of the church does not have a problem with an emphasis on sex. The world's perspective tends to overemphasize; however, **in the church, there is a tendency to downplay its importance.**

If **God has set sexual intimacy as one third of the foundation for marriage, (see Genesis 2:24)** then our doing of things must attempt to comply with His Divine design. We do realize that we may not hit perfection 100% of the time, life being life, but it must be in our thinking and planning so that we don't drift off into some crazy holding pattern that becomes detrimental to our wellbeing. Remember our illustration of the three-legged stool. Even if we are able to temporarily balance that stool on two of its legs, eventually it has to rest on three. That's the design! I know a lot of people don't understand it or believe it, but sex in marriage is there and there for a reason. God has planned it that way from the beginning. Ignore it and it has the negative power to destroy a marital relationship.

Enid and Frank have always been a wonderful example for many. Their love for each other has been legendary for almost 15 years. They are everywhere it seems and participate in everything. Both of them can be seen at PTA meetings, neighborhood improvement gatherings, town watch, and so on and on. They never seemed to stop. The problem is they've allowed themselves to be so busy that there is little time for their personal selves. When there is some time, they are too exhausted to even make the approach. Again, remember the Bible verse that says it takes time to be holy. Well **if God instituted and ordained <u>the marriage act</u>, then it is sacred.** It *should not be altered or put on hold.* Other things should go on hold. But definitely not that!

Frank's parents live about 15 minutes away and Enid's parents are about a half-hour away. Both sets of grandparents would be more than willing to help out with caring for their three grand boys. Joe, Frank's dad, is a former athlete and would be glad to take the boys to sporting events. Enid's parents are genuine nature buffs. They enjoy weekend camping trips, fishing, and nature hikes. Using their family resources would greatly help to open personal downtime to this couple. They both have siblings living near them which offer even more potential resources for taking romantic breaks. The real struggle is to get this couple to see that their relentless volunteerism and overwhelming devotion to their three sons is killing their romance. With their romance dying, their sexual intimacy is on the skids as well.

In any marriage, sexual intimacy has to be intentional. It cannot be left solely to spontaneity alone. Spontaneity is good, but waiting around for, *"those moments that are just right"* as one television commercials suggest, may come too few and far in between. **Love takes work. Romance takes work.** *Sexual intimacy should result from that same love and romance.*

I think that there are several categories of sexual intimacy that married people experience. Not every encounter is going to be fireworks, which is our first type. There are those special times when the heat is on and it is so wonderful and almost overwhelming. It would be great if it could always be like that, but that will not be the story every time. There are many articles featuring and encouraging simultaneous climax, trust me that will not always happen, but does not have to put a damper on the mutual enjoyment of a married couple. If it happens, it happens! Climax does not have to be the only point of satisfaction. **Don't ruin your total enjoyment because you did not** experience a sexual pot of gold. **Appreciate what you have had and move on for another day.** So, we could list *fireworks without mutual climax as a second category*. Category *number 3, I call maintenance sex*. It is more like, just because we need to do it. We need to connect regularly. Those are the times when it is not particularly special but we need to connect. It can be enjoyable, relaxing, and all of that, but no remarkable spark. **It is OK to have unremarkable intercourse with your spouse some of the time.** However, we should plan for and expect those fireworks moments.

John's and Erica's sex life had become dull and boring, to put it mildly. They had become so busy that they were just not interested in each other sexually after a while. They started to actually avoid each other. Then the sniping began. They became so cold toward each other and then the blame game. My question for them became, *"How much sexual intimacy are you having?"* Then came the blank stares, the fidgeting, and then the, *"Uuuummms…"* **Simple to understand, "There's no oil in the engine!"**

To deny one's spouse sexual celebration **unreasonably**, is to sin against that spouse. I believe that God looks at this as seriously as He does any other sin. Sin is sin! Let's look at the word **unreasonably** as it pertains to sexual intimacy. Please understand, once again, I am not talking about instances of illness, occasional times of exhaustion, a wife's cyclical period, or any other valid reason that may cause a brief time of reluctance or avoidance. Usually it is something physical but could be mental as well. I need to be sensitive here because I don't want to send a wrong message or set limits based on what comes from my thoughts only. I do understand that there are those occasional times when a spouse just may not be able to perform. This is to be expected in the life of human beings.

Just as I stated earlier in this book, my concern centers on the normal times when a couple could be and should be intimate. When Barbara and her husband suffered a miscarriage, it was understandable that they might want to spend time to heal mentally and spiritually along with physical healing for Barbara. This would be normal. What was not normal was her insistence that they not share sexually for 5 to 6 months after their tragedy.

The point is, if you are married, you cannot arbitrarily decide not to be intimate with each other. Once again, to make the point from another angle, to do this is sin according to the 'Marriage Manual!'

We do need to spend some time talking again to those who do have genuine sexual challenges. The question is what if you are unable to function in this area of your marriage is this against God's will? **When situations rise beyond our control and there is no intentional avoidance,** first we need to say that **there is no sin there.** If the problem is because of physical discomfort, be aware that we are living in the times of great medical enlightenment. I believe that God has invested a great amount of ever-increasing knowledge into the mind banks of medical practitioners. I also believe that if you are facing sexual challenges that there are expert physicians out there who can help you. Also, in the case of mental barriers there are people trained in mental disorders to help guide patients into a more comfortable mental climate. If you are a Christian having concerns about the kinds of counseling available there are serious and committed individuals who love the Lord and are equipped to give valued help and advice. Please do not give up. Help can be on the way.

I want to be consistent once again, If God has given us this beautiful gift, it is not unlikely for Him to supply the answer to our problems. Yet it is incumbent upon us to do everything in our power to find a cure. **Don't give up, don't give in and don't get bitter. <u>Seek diligently for God's way</u>!**

If God has given us the incredible gift of sexual intimacy, He must have a way for us to fulfill that gift. **It starts with prayer**!

WHAT ABOUT THE USE OF SEXUAL PERFORMANCE DRUGS, HERBS, OR MEDICINES?

A friend asked me a few years ago what I felt about those people needing chemical help to perform sexually. His concern was that he had a blood pressure problem and needed something in his system to maintain an erection. To be honest, I don't recall the Bible speaking about this at all, so I see no reason to prohibit someone in need of getting help.

When the Bible is silent on a subject, my recommendation has always been that we have to be very careful not to inject personal opinion and try to make it sound like the Bible. There may be those sexual things that are personally unacceptable to you and your spouse, that's ok, but don't try to imply biblical authority when it is not there. **God speaks when He wants to speak. When He is silent, shut up, and don't try to speak for Him!**

May I tell you that I shudder when I hear people thank God for giving them special insight that may not be universal in its application and appreciation. Your epiphany may be for you and not be a universally shared fact. To go ahead and publicly thank God for something that comes to one's mind, as though it is a divine edict from above is just not fair. Principles are understood from a universal perspective. Again, throwing a coin into the air will universally see that coin at the end of its trajectory, whether in India, Africa, or America, begin to plummet downward. We say that is gravity at work. It is a physical principle. What goes up must come down. Not 92% but 100% of the time. Spiritual principles work with the same kind of consistency.

ARE THERE RELIABLE PRODUCTS THAT DO NOT CROSS BIBLICAL LINES?

The following mentioned products are shared for their informational value only. Naming them in this instance does not in any way imply product endorsement, or usage recommendation. Viagra, Cialis, and Levitra are modern medical advances for men. There are other products such as Lyriana, Vigorelle, and Provetra that have been designed to help provide sexual enhancement for women. One might do well to checkout Google and Bing for other reference guides. Remember much of this cyber space information is based on the opinions of the general public, mixed with some experts' insight, but not always a reliable source.

In product usage, most people either have, or develop personal likes and dislikes based on who they are. Using any of these or any other products is certainly left up to the individual couple. On the other hand, I can see no spiritual or moral reason for one not to use them if they are needed or desired. **The caution is as always, 'Never abuse anything' and 'be careful of anything that drastically changes the natural body harmony or structure!'**

WHAT ABOUT EATING CERTAIN FOODS AND USING SOME HERBS TO INCREASE LIBIDO?

Some people feel rather uncomfortable using chemical helps to aid them in their sexual performance. Many couples have turned to using special foods and herbs to stimulate and enhance their sex experience. Does the Bible support or condemn this kind of practice? It may surprise some people to learn that special foods and herbs for sexual enhancement have been used throughout biblical history.

As far as I can see there may not be a direct mention of any foods intended as aphrodisiacs in the scriptures. However, Mandrakes are mentioned a couple of times and this type of fruit is listed as being an aphrodisiac on a few modern lists. Isn't it surprising that there is no mention of chocolate in the scriptures! Well anyway we will move on.

If you read The Songs of Solomon you will find a whole lot of what could be thought of as aroma-therapy listings. Things like myrrh, frankincense, aloes, spices, spikenard, honey and milk, saffron, and cinnamon, to name a few.

Clusters of grapes, pomegranates, apples and figs also seemed to be favorites of the two lovers in the Song of Solomon. Old Solomon and the beautiful Shulamite bride knew how to set the mood alright! That was long before aroma-therapy was an actual term.

If you wish to know more about the modern list of helpful foods and herbs, then the internet may be helpful. Try to a search on Google on *foods and herbs for sexual enhancement,'* on your computer. There are quite a few interesting things there along with explanations of what they should do. You could spend hours researching. One interesting thing I learned was about **Vitamin E.** Some like to call it the *"sex vitamin."* **The warning again is** *to be careful about all internet information since you cannot always be for certain of accurate or credible documentation or informed on the level of expertise or the intent of those sharing information.* Yet I think there is enough reliable information available for one who is discerning to gather intelligently.

It also makes sense to say what works for one person or couple may provide a complete turn off for another person or couple.

WHAT ABOUT THE USAGE OF CERTAIN PHYSICAL PARAPHERNALIA TO AID IN A COUPLE'S SEXUAL PERFORMANCE?

Some have asked about the use of sex toys in a couple's sexual celebration. I think the general rule should be that whatever is done should be in harmony and done in love. Even the condom industry has gotten deeply into the mix with the "ruffles and ridges" products. A bevy of colors and textures are now available. They come with reservoirs and without. Remember though, whatever you are planning should be to the mutual pleasure of both spouses and never outside of that mutual harmony.

The problem that I see with some of the advertised sex toys is that their usage could likely break the natural flow of mutual intimacy and divert the attention toward the individual. This would hamper mutual intimacy. While I am not categorically condemning the usage, I am suggesting extreme caution in their selection and usage. Some of the suggested stuff is just plain disgusting. It does not come anywhere near what God has designed. The real deal is that God has already equipped us with just about every natural apparatus we need to bring on sexual stimulation and mutual pleasure.

Again, the use of sex toys may help to limit the natural imagination and creativity that a couple would ordinarily develop together as loving partners.

Therefore, I strongly believe that there are elements that clearly cross the line. The use of instruments that could bring harm to the body, or the mind, or even the spirit, is far from what is acceptable. We hear that there are people who like to use stuff that will produce thoughts of horror and physical abuse. I am very sure that God is not going to be pleased with that kind of psychotic behavior. He presented sex as a gift, not a source of horror or abuse.

WHAT ABOUT SPOUSES PARTICIPATING IN SEXUAL ROLE PLAY?

Again, I think placing standards of good taste should be exercised in the privacy of their space where lovemaking among married people gets to make up their own rules. Some of the guidelines should involve privacy, safety, reasonableness, and mutual respect. Even fantasy and all forms of role-play should follow the above guidelines. **The bottom line at the end of the day is that both partners had clean fun and no one was compromised, or embarrassed, or in any way made to feel bad or guilty.**

After years of boredom and frustration Mary Beth Morgan, author of The Total Woman, greeted her husband at the door dressed only in high heels and a short apron. She wanted to turn the flames of their love life to hot. Boy did she get Mr. Morgan's attention. Her actions changed him from a very dull man into a dynamo by taking him off guard with her appearance. From that day forth, he never knew what to expect. But she later warned in her book to be careful to make sure that it is your own husband that you are opening the door for! Wow, I wonder what really happened there.

Remember privacy, safety, reasonableness, and mutual respect is the way to go. My friend Brian told me about a couple he learned about from an EMT worker. The story goes that this certain wife was bored with their sex life so she thought of how they could spice it up. She wanted her husband to dress up like Superman. So, he went out and found a costume, cape and all. She asked him to tie her to the bed post before he put his costume on which he did. After he changed, she screamed for Superman to come and rescue her. He ran out of the bathroom spun around, Superman style, and leaped up onto the bed, to save his damsel in distress. What he did not realize at the time was that there was a ceiling fan above the bed. When he jumped up the fan caught him in the head and knocked him out cold. There he lay unconsciously, bleeding profusely, and the woman helplessly tied to the bed. She screamed this time for real, trying to get some serious help. Help did not come quickly. When the Medics finally arrived, they had to break down the door. You can imagine their amazement to find a fully nude woman tied to the bed and her bleeding husband, still out cold, dressed in a Superman get-up. **This was certainly a fantasy gone wild. What started out to be a lot of fun turned out to be extremely embarrassing.**

Yes, it was private but certainly not safe. If safety had been taken into account, I suppose that some might say it was not unreasonable or disrespectable. **Some things you just might avoid because of the factors that you cannot control.**

How about those stories of couples taking private pictures and videos of their love making, only to have it appear on some website? On the positive side, good old regular sexual intimacy helps married people keep their affections centered, and free flowing. It helps to keep the spiritual heart in a tender sensitive state. It provides healing and restoration for the soul. It is like oil that helps the life of married people flow. Surgeon, Dr. Mehmet Oz, who began his public media career on the Oprah Winfrey show, and now has become *"America's Doctor"*, offers a whole list of physical pluses resulting from marital intercourse. I recommend checking out his daily TV programs and his website from time to time.

SOME MORE POINTS TO PONDER

Intercourse is the highest expression of spousal love between married people. It is the simultaneous act of giv-

ing while receiving. Only God could invent something so wonderful! The vast wonderfulness of it cannot be genuinely experienced or duplicated outside of the marriage bed. **The Bible warns about one joining ones' body with someone who is not your spouse.** In harsh language it strongly instructs that **this act causes one to be linked to a harlot.** So, we go back to **Dr. Tim LaHaye's definition that the *'marriage act,'* or sexual intimacy, was invented for the benefit of <u>married people exclusively.</u>** People who are not married to each other may engage in the act of sexual intercourse but really cannot obtain from it the act of oneness intended. Only God can bring that about, and only on His terms!

Animals lack this kind of intimate recreational bonding because they only mate to produce offspring. This is true even in the family lives of those animals that bond for their entire lifetime. Recreational sexual intimacy is an exclusive gift from God to human beings. **In fact, the only communication that is higher than spousal intimacy through intercourse is that of the divine communication one can have with God through prayer and meditation.**

Regular sexual intimacy helps married couples keep their affection centered and flowing for them. It keeps the spiritual heart in a tender sensitive state. It provides healing and restoration for the soul. When a husband and wife practice sexual intimacy, it clearly provides another wonderful communication medium. Their love quotient raises them to a level beyond.

Remember these words of Jesus found in Matthew 19:5 which echoes Genesis 2:24, … *"For this reason, a man shall leave his father and mother and be joined to his wife, and the two shall become one-flesh. So then, they are no longer two but one flesh. Therefore, what God has joined together, let not man separate."*

When you marry, separation or divorce should never be an option in your mind. Just as you are in your natural life, becoming what you eat, the same applies in your emotional, spiritual, mental life. As stated elsewhere, your will determines how you will move. If when you open your eyes in the morning and say to yourself, *"I will have a bad day today, I can just feel it."* It is nearly certain that you have determined the way of the day. On the other hand, you can awaken and say, *"I am looking for a great day today."* With that attitude it is more likely that your day will be at least good if not great! The same way your marriage comments can become a predictor of how your relationship goes along. Those couples who get married and allow thoughts of divorce to constantly filter through their minds are more likely to be in a relationship debacle. Part of the problem occurs because the negative thoughts and words collect any extraneous negative data that comes along. The negative thoughts become magnets that will attract anything that will stick to them.

Patricia and Kenneth had a pretty good marriage going for a good number of years. Kenneth started hanging out with some guys on his job that where closet swingers. They began to ride him about his prudish ways, but he held fast to his spiritual beliefs in the sanctity of marriage. He should have gotten away from them, but they made him feel like there were things he needed to learn from them. Well unfortunately he became a dedicated disciple. They pointed out to him that there were some hot chicks in their office waiting for him to show them a good time. Kenneth fell for the bait. He started sneaking out to have drinks, and predictably, it led to him being sexually unfaithful. Once he got a taste of this wayward life, he couldn't let go. At first, he felt guilty about his double life, but then in his mind, he started to rationalize his affairs as being necessary to his manhood. After a while he convinced himself that he actually deserved this extra pleasure. He worked hard to provide for his family; shouldn't he get all the goodies he could get? The next step in his downward journey was the dissatisfaction with Patricia. He felt that she did not please him anymore! He created in his mind a general spirit of dissatisfaction. And besides she was always demanding something from him and expecting him to do major things in their family life. These outside women he was now running with ask him for nothing but a good time. He steadily became more and more dissatisfied with Patricia. One evening while at a dinner in honor of her birthday, he announced to her that he was filing for a divorce. She was shocked! She had been aware that something major was wrong in their relationship, but nothing like this. She pleaded to no avail but he told her his mind was made up.

The Turners' did divorce, but it did not go quite like he thought it would. He was prepared for a 50 / 50 financial settlement, but the judge did not see it that way. Kenneth barely got lunch money out of the deal. On top of that he discovered that his philandering rewarded him with a serious STD. When we see him these days, he is a broken man. He had it all but allowed his personal discipline to corrupt his treasure.

The Bible has a quick remedy for avoiding this kind of world shattering recklessness Proverbs 5:18 instructs us to *"Return (In your mind) to the (spouse) of your youth!"*, before reckless behavior destroys the hope of redemption. Yes, we are back to **the practice of controlling the will**.

Make the investment; safeguard as well as spice up your love life. **It is a private concern that should be defended from any outside opposing forces**. Avoid outside influences that do not hold marriage to the highest standards. People who don't respect what you have and what you are trying to build, I would strongly advise to let them go. They can't help you. Remember, some people really don't want your marriage to succeed. They themselves are miserable and would have you that way too.

The sexual portion of your marriage is as vital as well as the other factors in your relationship. Do not ignore it! Investment is a must.

Recently I decided to surprise my wife by attending a women's convention in Florida with her. When first asked to attend I just could not see my way financially. As the date approached, I said to myself, *"Why not make it happen!"* Money was still tight, and it was going to cost more now than the earlier opportunity, but after all, it was only money. I got on the internet, found a hotel that was a reasonable distance from the main hotel (Because that hotel was booked solid). I then purchased my ticket on another almost affordable air carrier and the timing was working. Now I had to request for help to guard my secret mission. The other ladies were brought into my plan so that her room arrangements were switched. On the departure date I dropped her off at the airport and said our tearful good-byes. I then slipped off to long term parking and took the shuttle back. My non-stop flight arrived actually ahead of hers and so did the other ladies' flight. So, I met up with them while they were waiting for Dot to arrive. Sequoia, the group planner, went to meet her getting off her plane, and walked her over to the other ladies. I hid behind a post and stepped out after she joined the group. They engaged in some gal talk and I just stood there. Dot looked up and saw me standing there and was shocked in disbelief! This whole event was recorded and shared on Facebook, thanks to Pastor Elsa Bass. The trip cost mega bucks but will always be a wonderful event in our memory.

Do things regularly to enhance your love connection. Go out on romantic dates, take trips, and try new things that are appropriate. Don't settle into the feeling that you always have to go to the same bedroom at the same time. Put variety into your marital sex life! Some of the reported appeal of outside affairs involved mystery and suspense. Variety and daring are also often seen in these negative situations. However, these same elements can be introduced and used in positive ways in a bona fide marriage relationship without shame. I heard a famous actress ask a female talk show hostess if she ever engaged in phone sex. The hostess was taken by surprise, but her stumbling answer was actually good, *"Wellllll yessss but, not outside of my marriage,"* was the reply! Good answer! She was having some private times with her husband. **Keep it in the union but keep it hot; that's the potent secret!**

FOR YOUR NOTES & REFLECTIONS

....

....

....

....

....

....

....

....

....

....

....

....

....

....

CHAPTER 10

Let's Keep It In The House

SEVERAL YEARS AGO, the governor of the state where my wife was born was discovered in an adulterous affair. He managed to create a tangled weave of deception that the press was all too willing to untangle. After he was caught, he began to supply all kinds of hidden information. It seems, according to him, there was not just one, but several affairs, undiscovered by the press. Again, according to the governor, none of these affairs were really sexual encounters. However, this current, very sexual one, was this time with a woman in another country. This was different he felt. He went on to say that he discovered that this Argentinean woman was his soul-mate. In fact, after getting caught in this crazy affair, he wanted to try to fall back in love with his wife.

What in the world is going on in the governor's head? For starters someone needed to tell him, mixed up as he is, he does not receive a free pass to claim that this new woman is his soul-mate. His wife of 20 years should have been the only mate holding his soul. He along with too many others have it twisted; 'Soul-mate', which is not a biblical term, even though I do understand the term, cannot be used loosely to cover your sins outside of your marriage bed. But 'Soul Mate', is not, and cannot be some kind of entity that can be entered into and exited from, at will, with whomever.

Come on 'Gov', your commitment is real flaky. You could not have a soul-mate and a wife. Your spouse is your soul-mate. You don't just discover one along the way. In fact, spouses grow into that type of relationship. Soul-mates are made not found! As partners journey through life together they are forged into a closeness that makes it seem like their very own souls are knitted or welded together. That does not happen across some bar, dance floor, or hotel room shared by strangers. When I hear married people using terms like 'Soulmate' to describe someone other than their spouse, I know immediately that this person is looking for some kind of escape clause (I called them in an earlier chapter, **'*a gapfiller*'). Your commitment is your commitment! There is no moral/spiritual room for ducking out on your commitment.**

I'm sure you will agree that no couple standing before a marriage altar knows exactly what will happen in their future. It is there that the vows to love each other, *"for richer or poorer, in sickness and in health, until death parts the union"* are made. These vows are made in hope and faith. We cannot see ahead the way that time and destiny will deal with us. That handsome man in his early twenties with a full head of curly dark hair and wonderful strong muscles may in several decades be somewhat shorter with almost no hair on his head and too much unwanted hair sticking out of his ears and nose. It is quite likely that the beautiful young woman in her early twenties will several decades later not look any more like a model but instead have some sagging skin, unwanted fat, varicose veins, and traces of cellulite. No one enters into marriage knowing what they are going to look like in twenty years or have pre-knowledge about the many experiences they will have during their journey. Those kinds of thoughts and images just do not enter our minds before we get there. I sometimes now stare at the old man in the mirror staring back at me. Black hair, bright eyes and tight skin have all changed. I'm not even sure when it began to change. I was just living my life one day at a time. But the reality is that inside I am pretty much the same man I've always been. Should my wife decide to change her commitment to love me because my body shape, hair and eyes have changed? What if it takes me a nanosecond longer to recall something that twenty years ago would have been right on the tip of my tongue? I am essentially the same man I was back then. I would hope that my life experience has made me an enhanced version of myself. But all in all, the commitments we made at the altar on that beautiful day are to stand firm for the rest of our time. *Thank, YOU JESUS!*

We may have said at the time the required wedding vows as part of the ceremony. God took those vows seriously. He did not take them as some anxious, idle words, which were repeated because we were caught up in the thoughts, festivities, and events of the moment. Yes, marriage vows are never to be taken lightly when we make them, and how we play them out in life. Marriage is a serious business.

The Governor was probably committed when he was standing at the marriage altar. I think most people are at the time, but somewhere along the journey wrongful temptation and opportunity presented themselves. Somewhere in those moments he decided that his selfish personal desires were more important than the promises he made to his wife. **Temptation can come to anybody. Yielding to temptation is where sin reigns!** Sin is designed to bring ruin to the life of the already fallen. The devil likes to give the knife an extra twist.

The Bible again, in the book of Proverbs 7:21–27 helps us not to fall into stupid traps that lead to our destruction:

> *21 With her enticing speech she caused him to yield, with her flattering lips she seduced him. 22 Immediately he went after her, as an ox goes to the slaughter, or as a fool to the correction of the stocks, 23 Till an arrow struck his liver. As a bird hastens to the snare, He did not know it would cost his life. 24 Now therefore, listen to me, my children; Pay attention to the words of my mouth: 25 Do not let your heart turn aside to her ways, Do not stray into her paths; 26 For she has cast down many wounded, And all who were slain by her were strong men. 27 Her house is the way to hell, Descending to the chambers of death.*

When temptation comes it is not about how strong one is. It is more like how fast one can run. The act of running is admitting that there is a challenge. It is admittedly a soft spot that needs some intervention. To stand there repeating to yourself, *"I must not yield, I must not yield, I must not..."* will likely traumatize, rather than empower. Again, remember in the Bible *Joseph ran from his master's wife's advances.* From our cultural, oral tradition they used to say, *"A good run is better than a bad stand".* Now I'm very much aware of the scripture that says, *"Be strong in the Lord and in the power of His might."* This scripture encourages us to rely on a safe position within the power of the Lord; which is more than reliable. However, there is another scripture that encourages us to, *"Run with patience,"* which speaks more of method than position. Let me put these two scriptures together in paraphrase for us. *"Be confident in the power of the Lord for He will provide for you a steadiness as you run along patiently as He continues to provide that running guidance."* Learn to move out of harm's way, rather than trying to prove how strong you are.

Throughout all of my writings and teachings I have maintained that God set this world up to run by principles. Principles are universal moral and physical factors that are set up not to change. Gravity is the same whether you are standing on a windowsill in New York City or on a mountain in Nepal. Gravity pushes things down not up. If you ignore this principle, whether you happen to like it, or not, there is a consequence to pay for violating it. Moral/spiritual adultery is a line not to be crossed. Ignore the principle and consequences follow.

Sometimes consequences don't come right away but eventually they will come. Following our former governor's public outing, came the news that one of the countries' beloved and respected athletes was discovered shot to death in a house along with a female thought to be linked to him romantically.

People could not believe the report because he had such a fine reputation for community work. He gave a large sum of money to several charities. He not only gave money but he loaned his celebrity for many causes. He was thought to be a family man, with a wife and sons. The details were slow and cloudy at first, but not for long. The woman was established as his lover who had days before purchased a hand gun. Something happened in her mind and she shot him several times in his sleep, and then turned the gun on herself. Prior to this, he had bought his mistress an expensive SUV. Before the incident, unsuspecting neighbors and observers thought the couple was pretty happy. What a tragedy. Why did this man go out of his safe house into the arms of a woman who would take his life? Well, I don't know the whole answer, but one thing is certain, this athlete seems to have had the world in his grasp but **he devalued the real riches that he had.** His wife may have had some differences with him from time to time, but she never killed him.

There is another verse of scripture that says a man should drink water out of his own vessel. **Value what you have! Commit to making what you have work for the good!** Failing to see and appreciate what you have will lead to unrest, and disappointment. It is easy to look over the fence and assume that the neighbor's grass is greener. Taking it a step further by wandering over into the neighbor's yard, sitting down and claiming it to be yours is going to lead into some real conflicts. **The better solution is to fertilize your own grass.**

King David could have had almost anything he wanted. Why did he decide to choose to take Uriah's wife? In those ancient times if she was unmarried, he could have added her to his bevy of wives. But he was told from the gate that she was another man's wife. She was beautiful, and he was selfish!

Neither of these factors was a good reason for adultery. There is no acceptable reason for this act. But David chose to jump headlong into the thing that would change his life and the lives of countless others. That day a king was turned into an adulterer, a conspirator, and a murderer. Violate a principle and a negative consequence will follow. The string of misfortune did not stop even with the death of the child that resulted from that tryst on the roof. From that day on God placed a sword over the house of David. All kinds of peril historically took place in his household. Peace never prevailed in David's house again. What a price to pay for a moment of selfish fun.

Another biblical principle that affects not only life in general but marriage as well, is to actively avoid (*turn away from*) the appearance of evil. Both Proverbs 3:7 and I Thessalonians 5:22. Say pretty much the same. Don't play with it, avoid it!

Over the last 3 or 4 years I have been getting some troubled counselees whose' marriages are on the line because of cell phones and emails. I don't recall the Bible entering into the technical world of these modern-day utilities. But if you think about it, the principles governing their usage should line up with scriptural wisdom. The principle still holds true even concerning new things. More often the complaint comes from the wife who cannot understand why her husband has all those phone numbers of mysterious females in his directory? Then there are some men who think it is clever to list numbers without names. Hey Einstein, that does not help her feel better. In fact, that makes it worse! Then some of these wives don't stop at cell phone investigations, they go in and search email accounts as well. Again, some of these brilliant guys put passwords on their stuff. If you have to hide it, it should not even be there! That's like waving a red flag in front of a charging bull. No pun intended.

Now I do get around to reminding the wives that there is a "*Right to privacy*" issue here, and that to read someone else's email is not a right, or right to do. But please hear this *Captain Techno*, if you want a happy home, don't try to stretch this right to privacy issue too far with your wife! ***I'm just saying!***

I keep making the point that men and women are different. Most of the husbands tell me that it is no big thing. So then why are you sitting here in my office in big trouble next to your wife who looks like steam is coming from her ears? I want to yell out at you Mr. Clueless, ***"Are you insane?"***

These poor guys are just not thinking like their wives. No woman is going to put up with her husband spending social time with some other woman. Your wife wants your time!

Then some of these husbands have been discovered sharing real personal stuff. You just can't do that. Phone sex has crossed the line. Just in case no one else has ever told you that!

The mayor of one of our large cities was recently dethroned from the job because his text records showed that he was saying very, very intimate things, actually very nasty things to his female chief of staff. The phones that they were communicating on were paid for by the tax payers. The opposition was out looking for things to bring him down and they found it. His texting habits did him in big time! Dumb, Dumb, Dummmmb!

After our counseling sessions several of my guys claim that they told the women to stop calling them, but they were still getting calls and text messages. Since the females refused to stop, I felt that the most natural thing to tell them to do was to change the number and then refused to give it out to the cell abusers. Well, you would have thought that I had told them to step out in front of a speeding car. Now I understand to a degree, the difficulty in doing that. I've had the same cell number for over a decade. I would hate to change. But if that number became a problem in our relationship, I'm sorry, the phone number would have to go. One of the husbands went to the trouble of changing his number and lost no time in giving the new number to the woman that caused the office visit in the first place. Not too bright a decision brother. Get rid of the outside woman, or women in your life. Old School used to call them, *"Home wreckers"*. This guy was actually very bright indeed; he just did not want to hurt the woman's feelings. Hey if she could not abide by your request to stay off your phone, then she was not a real friend anyway.

Sometimes the question comes up whether one can have friends of the opposite sex and maintain a happy marital relationship? It all depends on the marriage itself and the friends we are talking about.

I have some very close female friends, but they happen to be just as close to my wife. We can talk for extended conversations, but they are open conversations, and always with my wife's knowledge. She is free to pick up the phone, which she rarely does, at any time. I never say anything to them that I could not say in front of my wife. They do not say anything to me that they would not say in front of her. We share no private secrets. Sometimes during the call, it is likely that these friends and my wife will talk to each other. Her friends are my friends. My friends are her friends. At some time in the process of life we get to choose who our close friends are.

Douglas and Ellen each had their own set of friends. These friends were always separated and never did any things together. So, this developed overtime a lot of secrecies. Suspicions of unfaithfulness, etc. floated around. Who knows if any of it was true? However, their marriage could not survive all of the drama. Unfortunately, it folded in the heat of the struggle.

Keep in the house those things that help to build your house. Keep your affections on God, and on each other. Build your house. Keep it in order. Shut out the extraneous things of the world that will not prove helpful to what you are trying to do. Only those persons who have an interest in helping to support what I am building are allowed to have any effect on my house. This determination covers the relationship in our marriage and even with how we raised our children. Once a neighbor came to lecture us on not giving our daughter enough freedom to party and mix socially, etc. We were polite but determined to stay the course we had set. Bottom line, our daughter did fine, and this women's daughter not so good!

Honor the Lord and His presence, and He will keep you in His perfect peace!

Amen!

FOR YOUR NOTES & REFLECTIONS

....

....

....

....

....

....

....

....

....

....

....

....

....

....

CHAPTER 11

Your Wife Wants You To Know

SOMETIMES HUSBANDS ARE simply baffled when it comes to understanding their wives. The problem often stems from the husband trying to figure it out from his own male perspective. Here's a news flash: **Men and women are different!** *"Wow"*, you say, *"How did you come to that astounding conclusion"*? Well, I am not trying to tease you with that statement, just trying to confirm what you've always felt.

Rev. Jeannette Flynn, the former Director of Kingdom Ministries of The Church of God, shares this little personal history. When she was getting married, her husband Chuck wanted to show his love for her so much that he could hardly wait to give her a special wedding gift. She began to open the pretty box as he stood looking on anxiously. Once she got into the big box her once gleeful spirit melted. What she discovered in the box was not some beautiful, personal, gift, but instead, a cooking pot. To Chuck this practical gift would make his new bride so happy. It was understandably difficult for Jeannette to hide her disappointment. She knew that he wanted to do something wonderful for her. Just at that time in life he didn't have a clue. She told me that they still, many years later, laugh about that gift.

The great reality is men and women, are wired differently causing us often to be very different in how we think about things, or how we react to them. Sometimes, even with the same stimuli, because of that intricate male/female wiring system, we may see differently, triggering different reactions.

Husbands learn pretty quickly that the things that stimulate them sexually are probably not exactly the same things that motivate their wives. It is pretty commonly known that most men are highly stimulated by what they see. Some experts have guessed at an 85% rate of response through the eye gate for men. This is one of the major reasons why the pornography industry has taken off at such an alarming rate. Guys like to see it in their heads. Of course, this is not always good because generally speaking, it is not their wives that they are viewing in their heads, but some substitute body, which is bound to take them off of the real mark. The Bible has a remedy when it tells us to, *"Enjoy the wife of our youth,"* Proverbs 5:18, and then in Ecclesiastes 9:9 it says, *"Enjoy life with the woman whom you love all the days of your fleeting life..."* and Prov. 5:15 *"Drink water from your own cistern* (faucet) *and running water from your own well.*

I believe these passages of scripture are pointing to the same triggering mechanism that causes the disconnection. Returning to the wife of our youth is a very strong urging from God, to return our minds to the original beauty that captivated us in the first place. God knew that part of the human makeup was curiosity. The mind has the ability to wonder, then wander, without discipline. These passages along with Malachi 2:14, instruct us to set our inner eye on a fixed target. That target is your wife's body as it was in its' prime. It is a clear call back to that moment in time, when you desired her the most.

Curiosity will tantalize and intrigue us into imaginary adventures. Once these forbidden adventures occur, they paint indelible photographic pictures on the walls of the mind. These pictures can unfortunately form a type of permanent file that can come open at almost any time. These visual/mental files tend to force us to make comparisons with what we should not have seen. The more you see, the more opportunities there are for these comparisons to float to the surface. If we are to overcome this dreadful state, we must be led back out of the same door that provided entry. It must be the willful turning, and convincing of the personal mind.

Comparing your wife to some electronic image is totally unfair to her. She was made by God and given to you for your enjoyment and satisfaction for a lifetime. Actually, she was uniquely designed for you. Also, it should be said that you were designed for her.

I don't think that I've ever talked to a Christian man who did not admit that he knew that pornography was wrong and against God's plan for his life. The problem is that most who have fallen into this abyss were led captive through their curiosity. Curiosity is like holding onto a string that never allows you to reach its' end on its' own.

The antidote for this behavior, beside genuine prayer, is complex. But in the mix of things a change of mind/heart and a raw determination to exclude all others must be there. Remember, what you have is what you have. **Appreciate what you have.** Set your affections on those things that are at your hand. **Be satisfied with what God has given you.** *These are the first steps of turning away.*

It is very likely that your wife will never be able to perform in some of the positions that you have seen in cyberspace or in video trysts. Please know that what you have probably seen is staged. It's just drama! These folks make money by exciting their viewers. It does not have to be real, just exciting. More than likely in their private sexual lives they are not performing as they do on camera. I wish that I did not have to tell you to think about it, but for the sake of argument, some of these things presented are just plain dumb and would lack any level of real-life comfort. Remember the industry is growing on unrealistic fantasy. The love of money is the root of all evil.

John wanted his wife Susan to dress up and pour stuff on him, etc. Where did he get this from? He got the idea from something he saw. Susan tried to comply with some of the stuff he requested but most of it was just plain ridiculous. It was novel in a sense but ended up so uncomfortable that neither of them enjoyed the moment. It was a total waste of time plus the extra clean-up. John's insistence that they follow this route made his wife feel that she was not good at meeting his needs. Struggling with all the other things that married people struggle with, she could now add a measure of lowered self-esteem to her list.

Your wife does not want to be compared with some image that you saw somewhere and now is stuck in your overdrive. She probably has her own struggles with her weight and how she looks. **She does not need you to come along and try to mold her into a hooker wannabe.** She wants you to know that it is hard for her to satisfy herself in her own view. If she has given birth it is likely that there are bulges and patches of unwanted fat that she tries to deal with; and often dealing not too well either! If she is beginning to age, even the slightest bit, she is waging a constant warfare on body spread, and wrinkles, and gray hairs and on and on. The very last thing she needs is for the man in her life to show dissatisfaction with the very thing she is already battling. **She needs your support not your condemnation.**

Larry's eyes followed and dwelled too long on every shapely young woman that passed him. It was not even that he was appreciating the passing woman's appearance but his gaze seemed to indicate that his thoughts were going much further and deeper than appropriate. Jenny felt that each time it happened it was a direct rebuke of her, and the more than 35 pounds she had gained after having their two children. She tried hard using several popular diets but the weight kept on coming. Because of his implied rejections of her, she ate to medicate. Inside she was still the wonderful woman he married. Larry's carelessness is very crucial. It affects the next steps toward if, and how, Jenny recovers her selfesteem. Actually, Jenny should know that Larry's roving eye has nothing to do with her weight. Larry has to deal with some internal character issues.

Wives are generally stimulated more by acts of kindness and tenderness. In my second book, **MARRIAGE: The Rules of The Game**, I make a real point about the acts of kindness and tenderness, coupled with supporting deeds. In fact, I believe it is so powerful please allow me to quote extensively from chapter 6.

Generally speaking, kind words, tender touches, and supporting deeds stimulate most wives while most husbands are turned on visually. The great mistake that many husbands make is in thinking that since we are turned on visually that our wives are stimulated in the same manner. The sight of fancy lingerie is more of a guy turn-on thing than it is for women. Certainly, most women like receiving gifts and the look of pretty things, and perhaps even the thrill of light filmy garments touching them, but remember, the turn-on is a male thing. Her sexual stimulation comes from a far different source. Men can rise to the occasion quickly through the eye gate. We can become aroused at the drop of a hat. We could be compared to a racecar going from zero to 60 in a matter of a few seconds. Our wives are not like racecars but more like the old 'T model', and 'A model cars' that were patiently hand-cranked to turn the engines over. Then after cranking the engines they had to sit idling until they were warmed up.

*Almost every magazine these days features some headlined article on how to stimulate super erotic moments. "101 Ways to Turn Your Woman On"; "The Hidden Treasures of Intimacy"; "Fifty Ways of Love Making"; "Finding Her Secret Spot" ... on and on they go. Listen, you can pretty much save your money if you remember "WTD". <u>Kind words</u>, <u>tender touches</u>, and <u>supporting deeds</u>. This is shared because it is seen pretty much as a need that most women have. It is not shared to maneuver or manipulate. It just makes all the sense in the world that if it is a need that can be supplied easily by husbands, we should learn to build it into our regular routine. This is the formula that can make **you**, Mr. Husband, into Mr. Great Husband! Remember, **"WTD", kind words, tender touches, and supporting deeds.***

The words should be kind words of recognition and appreciation. Not words of ridicule and condemnation. Loving caring words that help her know that you value her greatly; words that identify her as the one closest to your heart.

What I can remember about the TV character Archie Bunker is that he almost never had any intentional, endearing words for his wife Edith. He ridiculed and put her down at every opportunity. The show's writers projected her even in the face of all the putdowns as a dutiful, jovial glutton for the punishment her husband gave. Remember now that was TV; it does not work in real-life. Trust me, Edith Bunker <u>does not live in your house</u>!

Positive communication in a loving environment is enhancing. I try to remember to always say thank you to my wife for cooking all of the great dinners she prepares. She goes all-out not only in the preparation but in the presentation as well. She decorates my plate the way a master chef would. She sees to it that the table is always set with a place-mat, etc. she loves it when I notice these things and say, "thank you." When we eat out, she always thanks me for dinner. Our love is regularly expressed with kind words, and loving deeds of appreciation.

A husband who learns and practices the art of soft words turns away wrath. Now when I say this, I am in no way suggesting or condoning dishonesty and subterfuge. What I am encouraging is that husbands should find the easiest and nicest way of communicating your heart. Then remember, don't let all of your conversations center around business, the bills, the kids, the house etc. Tell her the nice things about herself. Let her know how much you appreciate her; the sacrifices that she makes for you and the family. These are the things that most husbands receive and accept, but rarely really notice. If you begin to notice them it will put you in a different league altogether. The ultimate home run is when you make her feel good about herself. I haven't met too many women who are not concerned about their appearance. "Am I getting too heavy"? "Do you think I've lost too much weight"? "Is my hair getting too long ... too gray ... too dull", etc.? "What do you think about the way I dress lately"? The questions that wives ask about themselves never end. If the husband begins to volunteer compliments before the questions come, he will meet a deep need. When he begins to address her need for verbal reassurance, her appreciation level for him will increase.

I remember learning in the schoolyard that little poem/ motto that went, "Sticks and stones will break my bones, but words will never hurt me"! Now that little slogan helped get me through Elementary, Junior High and Senior High School, but beyond the school context, when you think of it the slogan is pretty dumb. Words can hurt! They may not have the ability to break bones but they certainly have the potential to break hearts. I think I even knew that back in kindergarten while being called some pretty awful names. The poem just helped to launch a counterattack so that the little perpetrator wouldn't know that you suffered a hit.

Yes, words can certainly hurt. That's why we caution couples to use the most positive words they can use in conveying a message.

The good news is that words can heal! I remember running to my mama after one of those schoolyard bullies sent a verbal brick through my poetic fence. But mama, before she did anything else, would sit me down and begin pouring on the verbal oil. She would remind me how special I was and that no one who really knew me could ever say something like that about me. Well, when I walked out of a private head session like that with Dr. Mom, I was ready to go back out on the battlefields of life. Her words healed me!

They not only healed me for that occurrence but put healing in me for a lifetime!

Husbands must be ever so careful to put healing into their wives. The secret is to place in them words that affirm them and benefit them before they experience an outside hit. Confidence builds walls that protect. Wives who feel protected and appreciated are far more likely to feel intimately aroused. Romancing her early in the day may set the kind of thrilling tone for her that escalates and expands through the day. Whether or not the marriage act is experienced that particular night is not of the greatest importance. Romance can be cumulative. It just may accumulate over a couple of days stirring up great sexual passions that explode into great moments for each of you.

----%%%%%%Taken from Marriage: The Rules of the Game %%%%%%----

Falling Back in Love Again

Again, we make the point that wives are generally stimulated more by acts of kindness and tenderness, coupled with supporting deeds.

Helen and John had been married for about seventeen years. They had three children, a nice home in the suburbs, and the normal debts that married people have. John started to notice that Helen had become very restless and dissatisfied about almost everything over the last several years. He tried to figure out where all of this negative stuff was coming from. Trying to fix the problem, he decided to pour money into their house and whatever else he thought he could do to satisfy her unrest.

One good thing that marriage counseling provides is a format to help people talk more freely. Married folks should make time to talk to each other but so often when something happens to block that freedom, it gets increasingly easier to build walls that separate. The next thing that usually happens after the wall starts is a tendency to justify why there is a wall.

After several sessions it was discovered that what Helen really wanted was for John to show more personal interest in her, not their house and other things. *"Take me out of here. Let me have a real life,"* she screamed at him one day. Finally, she was able to confess that she was feeling trapped. For most of the seventeen years she was having children and keeping house.

In her mind, John got to go out into the world and see things. To her, John's life was an ever-changing kaleidoscope of events. To her, life was centered around children, and house work. Trying to financially struggle to maintain the suburban dream limited their time and money to do other things. She felt that John never really took her out just to show her off. She felt that socially she had become a misfit. Maybe she had always been a misfit she began reasoning. She resented being defined solely on her mothering and domestic skills. She wanted John to love her for something else. She was intelligent, and gifted, but lately it seemed to her that all validity was based on the kids and home. It did not help her when even her church celebrated her as one of its' top moms of the year. Was she only a good mom? Was that the sum total of her existence?

What John could not see, was that she needed to be appreciated for her personhood, aside from the things she did. To base everything on her serving skills alone was shallow in her eyes. Yes, she really was a good mom, and a good wife who kept a good home, but that was what she did, not who she was!

What John could do to begin reversing some of her malaise is to begin simply looking at the things that she was complaining about. Use these things as road markers toward a different future. Rather than try to defend the things that irritated her, he could begin to highlight the things where she sought recognition. She wanted to be recognized as the beautiful woman in his life. She was discouraged about the few pounds that she had gained after giving birth to their three children. She was still a beautiful lady. Their comfortable home had become, for her, a private prison. John needed to celebrate her apart from their home. He had to begin taking her out to places where she could be noticed. In order to do this, he had to recognize that a wardrobe change was necessary. The clothes that she wore to PTA functions and even church services probably would not fit the bill.

Once he really got it, he began to reinforce his appreciation for her as a person. Instead of buying her toasters he started buying her dresses, jewelry and lots of personal things.

Helen needed his time. She began to enjoy sharing her thoughts about life and the ways of the world. He discovered that she loved to write poetry and had actually been doing it and tucking it away in all kinds of storage places. John began helping her to gather these gems of creative genius and fashioning them into book form. He found her a publisher and they launched an unexpected career.

Helen also began to show concern for their food diet. Rather than complain because they were beginning to eat differently, he offered no resistance. He even started going to the gym with her sometimes. John found that Helen seemed to appreciate him more as he began to soften his understanding of her. At one point she wondered who this new man in her life was?

FOR YOUR NOTES & REFLECTIONS

....

....

....

....

....

....

....

....

....

....

....

....

....

....

CHAPTER 12

Husbands and their Secrets

IT IS OFTEN said that women are difficult to understand. This is mostly said because women tend to change before their first pattern becomes what we thought was going to be a pattern. Confusing? Well yes, you've got the point. Just when you think that you have figured it out, with a woman, there is likely to be another wrinkle in the fabric. The good news for women is that this little confusing trait actually seems to draw men in like a moth to a flame. The mysterious ways of a woman both frustrates and delights us. I talked to a young husband whose wife was expecting. He was both frustrated and intrigued with his wife's crying. *"When I asked her, what is wrong she can't tell me."* *"Sometimes she is crying because she is sad, and sometimes because she is happy; but there is never a reason for either."* I just smiled and reassured him that everything would work out fine. I thought of Pastor Paul Earl Sheppard's recommendation that we all become panologists in our philosophical dealings with life. According to Pastor Paul, '*Panology*,' simply says that it will all pan out in the end! I told the young man to be patient and kind and as helpful as he could. Perhaps some of what he was experiencing was due to the pregnancy but it was not too far off from some of her regular behavior. I didn't want to tell him to stay tuned, because after the baby arrives would come a whole different set of emotions from his wife.

Now after having said all of that, let's realize that on the other hand, men have their own degree of difficulties. It is true that men tend to be a little more predictable in their behavior, but this does not at all explain our behavior. Honestly, we certainly can do some weird things too. For starters let's look at some of the toys and games men play with.

Dirt Bikes, Play Station, paint ball, Grand Theft Auto the list goes on, but I think you get the idea. Many of these toys and games are centered on aggressive behavior. We tend to like things that blow up and self-destruct. Don't overlook the growing fad of home theater rooms, and 'Man Caves'. Men are buying huge TVs and media screens with surround sound to do nothing more than to get the action up closer and louder to us. If it is going to blow up, we want it so up close and personal that it makes us flinch and duck for cover. Violence is not only tolerated it is expected. My wife and I have discovered recently that we cannot watch some types of movies together. I have no answer when she wants to know how I can stand to watch all those car chases and bullets flying. There is something really weird going on when you see the mildest of men watching the most violent movies.

Another strange question is: what brings on a mid-life crisis for some men? These men can go on through life without causing anyone to even raise an eyebrow, and suddenly, change overnight. Sometimes it is a change in wardrobe that signals us that something is going on. Some will remember in the 50's and 60's when some of the brothers began not buttoning most of the top buttons of their bold/bright shirts and added these large round PEACE signs around their necks. This jewelry was so large you almost wanted to pray that they would not fall face down off of the pavement into any running water in the streets. There was sure to be a drowning! Well, maybe it was not quite that large, but it was interesting.

Ronald was doing pretty well in life. He had a wonderful wife and a loving daughter. He was moving up the corporate ladder and the money was really good. Suddenly, he wanted to be a ladies' man. He picked up some willing woman and went through some kind of sexual escapade. Tiring of this first affair he started another, and then another. We lost count after that. He was finally discovered when his wife's friend Janice spotted him checking into a rather seedy motel where the friend did maid service. Thinking himself to be all of that, he lost everything.

Certainly, all incidents of mid-life crisis do not go into, or lead to affairs. The behavior can take many paths. Some men suddenly get interested in dangerous adventures, or sports that previously were not even anywhere on the radar. Why would 50-year-old Rodney, out of the blue, decide that he needed to become a race car driver?

My thoughts and observations lead me to believe that a midlife crisis in a male, signals some kind of personal unrest with ones' self. It probably starts with a man doing a selfevaluation that concludes with the thought that he has not done very much with his life up to that present time. It pushes on his mind that he needs to do something significant before it is too late. So then may come the plunge that seems to come from nowhere. He may feel that he is running out of time and needs to do it now. It is an inner crisis that might just be based on no facts at all, or on some inner longing to be heard, or seen, or anything. It may be, and usually is, all in the mind of the person. Others around may be completely satisfied with who the man is, or what he is doing. I think that it is very much related to that same lifelong drive that causes a man to *need to be respected* as a sign of love and approval.

More male weirdness can be noted when we see that the male brain can cause men to be turned on sexually, for no apparent reason. A piece of paper thrown across the room might end up producing a sexual thought. Even though you know that you, dear lady, are not turned on that way, don't forget that your husband is likely to be coming from a whole other direction sexually. You both must find a way to fulfill each other's legitimate sexual needs.

You know another area of strange behavior is that men tend to be very territorial. We read about men who fatally fight over a parking space. Recently in the Philadelphia area, two brothers in law, who happened to share the same house, got into an almost fatal fight during the democratic primaries, because one was a Hillary Clinton supporter, and the other a Barack Obama supporter. What were they thinking? Perhaps they were trying to lessen the vote by one? Yes, men do have some difficult issues to define manhood.

Maybe when men accuse women of being difficult to understand it is because of our own big bag of difficulties. It is just very different from what a woman is dealing with. We kind of miss each other in passing sometimes, maybe because we are concentrating on different things. Sometimes it can be like two trains passing each other in the night, going in opposite directions. Both on tracks right next to each other, and just as determined to reach the next station.

Sometimes it appears on the surface that we don't share the same emotions. Generally, it is thought that men don't cry. I'm not sure that is true of all men. I believe that all men at some point in life do some crying. What may be different about our wives, and to our undoing, is that much of our crying may be done on the inside. We tend to keep everything on the inside and this is not the healthiest thing to do. Women usually express outwardly how they feel on the inside. They are not ashamed to let their inner emotions out in the open.

In most of my early manhood years I don't recall crying much; especially with visible tears. However, I have noticed that as I've gotten older the tears flow much more easily. I now cry while watching touching movie scenes, and such things that play on the strings of my emotions.

Recently when Senator Barack Obama was elected to be the 44th president of our country I was away at a conference in Phoenix, AZ. That night, I was in my hotel room watching the world-wide celebration and I shed tears of joy; especially watching Rev. Jesse Jackson openly weeping on TV. But, two days later at the end of the conference, I listened to my friend Rev. Suzanne Haley address the large gathering of ministers from around the country. I could not help myself as I openly wept.

Suzanne spoke of her disappointment at not feeling like she could freely celebrate a great moment in history because the day before while the world was celebrating the historical victory, we in our National conference held in Phoenix, AZ were silent. The great historical event was not even mentioned publicly by our leadership. I know that the reason was that no one wanted to offend those that voted for the other candidate. However, Suzanne's challenge brought relief. That day I did not even try to wipe away the hot tears flowing down my cheeks. My soul needed some cleansing! It was a time to cry, and I saw others do the same.

Men on the surface may be warm and friendly, but that is usually as deep as it gets. You will need an extra special pass to see beyond the surface. After a while it becomes almost a natural thing to deal on the surface of things. We were either taught or learned in some way that it is *"manly"* to deal on the surface and hide our deeper feelings.

It is always interesting to me that women can go to the ladies' room and strike up a conversation with a complete stranger. It is not likely for men to do that. Generally speaking, men don't hold conversations in the men's room. Occasionally they may exchange a brief greeting grunt but rarely does it go any further than that. In fact, too much men's room conversation probably would raise a caution flag in some minds. It is somehow thought not to be very manly.

Taking it a level beyond Rest Room conversation, most men are very good at covering their emotions. Perhaps it is a learned response, or maybe a bad experience, that has taught us that showing any inner feelings is somehow going to detract from our manhood. So, we become experts at dealing on surface levels.

Yes, my dear sisters, please note this: Part of a man's wrapping is to cover up his inner privacy. He is not likely to be open about all the things he is feeling or thinking. It may in time come out of him in dribs and drabs, if you are patient. Again, generally, men are not very comfortable when they are badgered about the things hidden in their heart/minds. Notice that when men are troubled or cornered, they become almost monosyllabic. On the other-hand a sister may blurt out the whole thing while a brother will cut down to fewer words than usual. Don't mistake his lack of words as a sign that he is without thoughts. In fact, when men are silent it very well may signal that their thoughts are actually running deep. Remember there are usually layers involved. Think of it the way onions are constructed. Each layer down goes closer to the heart.

The secret to getting to a man's heart is listening carefully to the few words that he is offering. Accept these few words and pray for him. The likelihood of him telling you more is tied up in how you accept his limited early offerings. If you try to probe and pry it will likely push him the other way.

Men tend to be very egocentric. Because of this egocentrism they often link their manhood with situations and events. It may help a woman to understand this male ego trait if we compare it to how she feels about the acts and events that make her feel loved. Interestingly, this is the same way a man feels about his need to feel respected. Women need to feel loved like men need to feel respected. Love and respect are pretty much the same emotion, colored by gender. I like to refer to Proverbs 31:23 when making this point. Notice the reference to this wonderful woman taking special care to make sure her husband looked good in the gate. The background of this is that the city gate was like our modernday City Hall. It was there in the gate that all business was taken care of. I am pretty sure that marriages were arranged there; along with divorces and any other official things. This is probably where the major debates and lawsuits took place.

This was the place where public policy was set. Scriptural theology was handled here as well as mandating just how it was to be applied in the home. This lady was concerned about her husband's appearance in this special place and made sure that he looked good! We have a modern expression that may work here: *"Clothes that make the man"*. Perhaps a little shallow but does demonstrate a certain *esprit de corps*. She expressed her love by making him look good while he expressed his love by representing her well.

Hebrew/ Asiatic culture, which probably provided the back drop for the writing of Proverbs, allowed only the men of the city to officially gather in the gate. It probably provides an early look at what we now refer to as *"A good old boys club"*. Only the men of the town were invited. It seems that what women were facing biblically was a *"Stained glass ceiling"*. In today's world, I'm sure that this practice would not stand very long.

Although extremely partial to men, scripture does mention a woman named Deborah as a judge in Israel. Perhaps there might have been other women leaders, but I think that you get the point; it was thought to be a man's world. Unfortunately, this has carried over in some of our circles today.

Returning to the why factor in the statement about how her husband looked in the gate is very telling to how most men view their public persona. Most men like to be seen and seen in a certain way. Personally, even when I dress down, I want to achieve a certain signature appearance. I think it says volumes about me. Yet it is not saying that I only want to be seen wearing casual clothes, because when I want to dress up, I am interested in making a signature statement as well. I admit that I am complex, and I guess it only tells you who I am at that particular time. Having said all of that I'm not sure that men now in general, are vastly different about wanting to be seen.

Topping the factor of men wanting to be seen, is men wanting to be heard. Now I know that we have talked a lot about the silent male. Many men could have the motto, *"The fewer the words the better"*. However, this does not mean that they don't want to be heard. Not wanting to talk is different from not wanting to be heard. This is perhaps the factor that seems to derail some wives. The Proverbs 31 woman understood that her husband had to look a certain way in the gate in case he wanted to speak but by all means he needed to be heard. My late uncle Arthur was always interesting to me. He was a man of very few words. His wife Ruby usually did all the talking, but I always had the feeling that he was the one in charge. He was the silent type they refer to but he was certainly heard for sure. I have a good friend who happens to be a bishop. When entering a room full of clergy, a certain amount of attention and respect is accorded to him. It is not just because he is a bishop. His wisdom over the years has brought this kind of honor and respect. He really does not have to say a word. His presence speaks volumes. Should he decide to speak he definitely is heard by all in attendance.

Proverbs 17:28 says *"…and he that shuts his lips is esteemed a man of understanding."* Some have said that it is better to say nothing and be well thought of than to speak out of turn. One old adage put it this way, *"It is better to be thought foolish, than to open your mouth and confirm all doubt"*. I was looking at a news interview yesterday when the host asked his guest why he said he knew a certain group of men was lying? The reply was," *Because, I see their lips moving"*!

If you want to honor your husband listen to him, what he says, and does not say! Listen to his heart! Respect what he says *and he will talk to you more.* Badger him and he will likely retreat. **Let his few words have great weight**. Respect is not just a desire on his part, but it is needed. If you disrespect a man enough, he can feel defeat and failure. This is true especially if he perceives disrespect coming from someone on the inside. Wives occupy the first position in the man's heart, and then come the children. You must work hard at training the children in how to respect their father. You can also help him to posture himself to get their respect. Some men just don't get it. These guys could use a little help from you but be gentle is the way! Take care in guarding their most vulnerable place, a potential injured ego.

Inside of most men abides a champion, a **slay-a-dragon spirit**. Men want to conquer something and bring it back on their shoulders. This is part of a man's nature. Take that part of him away and you will see a man beginning to feel useless with feelings of failure looming near. Too much of these heavy feelings weighing him down and you can be sure that a state of depression will emerge. Men who are suffering can make unwise decisions and sometimes stupid choices.

Bennett was a smart guy who never felt quite comfortable with his wife's political career. She was not an actual office holder but was recognized all over the country for her political connections and her abilities to influence law makers. Bennett accompanied her on many of her speaking engagements. People would jockey for an opportunity to be in her presence on these occasions. Bennett would be somewhere twiddling his thumbs in a corner cringing, while trying to look important. The green-eyed monster was waging strong warfare on him and Bennett was losing.

In his wife's eyes he was appreciated for his companionship and what seemed to be support. April did not require him to be or do anything spectacular. She loved him just the way he was. They never talked about her career choices. She thought that everything was all good. But Bennett could never get over how he appeared to himself. *"I'm just the 'Go for' around here"*, he would often joke.

Many men in a similar situation have gone on to adjust or found a way of addressing the issues with their out-front wives. Many husbands who operate kind of shadowing their out-front wives have found a way to work out some kind of understanding, or even a compromise. Unfortunately, he did not. He began pursuing the interest of other women who did not have a rock star status. Eventually he allowed himself to drift into infidelity. These women were eager to massage his fragile ego. The devil set him up big time. He lost the love of his beautiful wife, his relationship with his teenage daughter, and on top of everything else, he contacted HIV Aids.

Let me quickly add, April was not at fault for the marital break down. Bennett allowed himself to be intimidated by her success. He should have seen it as their joint accomplishment. After all they were supposed to be one. Perhaps she should have seen some of the hidden divides in their relationship, but she didn't. He was not forthcoming at all. She loved him and really did value him, but he could not see himself as a worthy champion. What he told himself became louder than her words of appreciation. Scripture warns us that what a man thinks in his heart actually sets the stage for his own reality!

What your husband thinks about himself is important to his personal health. This encompasses mental, emotional, spiritual, and yes even his physical health as well. Many times, you, my lady, can hold the key. Remember that big guy with the voice deeper than yours, may be carrying around with him a less than strong ego. Archie Bunker may have picked on Edith because he was intimidated by her good qualities. What an interesting thought.

By now I have a few wives upset because of all of this emphasis on the man. Why is he so special, and what about the needs of the wife being heard? Well the name of this chapter is: 'Husbands and Their Secrets'. Did you miss it? I did my best for you in the previous chapter 11.

So, this is not about wives right now. Trust me, I'm trying to help you—not hurt you. I'm trying to help you get into your husband's heart. Just think about Aretha Franklin's song RESPECT. This will get you through that illusive door and into his heart. This is where you need to be if you are not. This is where he needs you most. Even if on the outside he has not realized it. Once you gain entry you are in a prime position to hear his heart. Again though, gentle is the way. Never malign or ridicule him for his thoughts. Listen and support, when, and where, you can. Once he senses your love and genuine support, he will safely confide in you.

Amen

FALLING BACK IN LOVE AGAIN

12 Steps to saving your relationship Reader insights:

MARTHA TUCKER'S REVIEW: *"Dr. David Stevens, pastor and marriage counselor seems to have put his finger squarely on the "Fix -it" button of the marriage, relationship, and dating world.*

In Dr. Stevens' book, **FALLING BACK IN LOVE AGAIN**, *the reader gets to look back at the love that once flared in their marriage. He helps couples recall the laughter, excitement, and ecstasy that thrilled their hearts in the early days. Dr. Stevens allows couples to linger a moment as a reminder of what they are trying to save.*

Additionally, readers come to understand differences in the sex drives of men and women and that it is all in God's design Dr. Stevens uses his book to make sense of differences that often dry up love and marriage. You might be surprised about God's plan!"

ONE OF DR. STEVENS' FAVORITE "FIX -IT" QUOTES

*"As a marriage counselor, I encourage people to **forget about trying to have a perfect marriage and strive to be perfectly married. This goal works to settle and narrow the "have-to-have-my-way"** divide. **What I have is what I have!** There is no need to look outside to find anything else. When you **believe that your spouse is perfectly suited to meet your needs, looking outside is not an option.***

"I think this may be the major factor for some people who cheat. **They refused to close the door on their relationship but keep foolishly looking for a "Gap-filler".** *That's a person who paints a fantasy that seems to look like they actually have that something that is missing in their relationship. This is how many couples get into trouble. Dr. Stevens shows how to activate the magic button of* **"forgive and forget"** *so they can move on to a much better relationship place.*

Readers were so pleased after reading FALLING BACK IN LOVE AGAIN, they wrote: *"I really felt the keen sense of Dr. Stevens' understanding of what was at stake in a failing relationship. He used seven good examples to show how a husband-and wife can meet somewhere in the middle without losing ground. I found his advice to be solid and helpful,"*

—Barbara Hall

"I felt that with the divorce rate being at 50%, this book could save couples tons of money if they want to salvage a relationship. We live in such callous times when love and commitment seem almost nonexistent.

—Marti Tucker

"*This book is full of 50+ years of wisdom, and creativity. Who wouldn't take loving advice from an author who has been happily, and successfully married for 50+ years? That alone tells me the advice in this book by Stevens has to work. It's a sure thing! Get the book, I promise you it will bless your relationship if you heed the instructions*".

—JANICE LAUDERDALE

ROCHELLE ROW writes: "*A word to us singles; <u>We need this book</u>! it is a great research and preparation tool for when our love interest comes along. "FALLING BACK IN LOVE AGAIN 12 Steps to Saving Your Relationship by Dr. David Stevens supplies valuable relationship principles whether one is married or single*".

<u>Editor's Note:</u>

Dr. Stevens' opinion after 50+ years of marriage counseling, **FALLING BACK IN LOVE AGAIN** must be based on trust. It is the key component to bringing relationship, passion and joy back into a struggling marriage or courtship. It lays out marital bliss accompanied by honest observation of both partner's needs and nuances, pointing out how each can find agreement. Dr. Stevens does not sugarcoat the issues.

He believes his wisdom can help save marriages. He encourages couples to find the options of compromise.

FALLING BACK IN LOVE, AGAIN instructs the couple to recall those pleasant memories of how their love began and to recapture the bliss and pleasures of the past.

He often quotes from the Bible which supplies multiple gemstones of wisdom.

"The best way to keep love alive is to feed it! Anything allowed to starve will die. Think of a fi re in an outdoor grill. As long as you keep adding charcoal briquettes, it will probably keep on cooking. If the fire is allowed to go completely out, then the only remedy is to start over".

***If your love has gone cold, do not delay or debate*—read the solid, easy and helpful strategies, and don't waste another moment wondering if it's the right thing to do. Regain your partner for years to come.**

FALLING BACK IN LOVE AGAIN
12 Steps to saving your relationship
By Dr. David R.L. Stevens

ABOUT THE AUTHOR

Rev. Dr. David R. L. Stevens is the senior pastor of Christ Center Church of God in Philadelphia, PA and has served the congregation for the past 55 years. He was ordained on September 14, 1969, by the Church of God, general offices in Anderson, IN and received his Doctor of Divinity Degree on June 6, 1981 from the Jameson College in Philadelphia, PA.

Before retiring from the School District of Philadelphia, Dr. Stevens taught in the Mentally Gifted Program. He currently serves as the Chairman of the Delaware Valley Pastor's Fellowship which started November 1969 and consists primarily of 18 senior pastors, and their associates within the tri-state area: Philadelphia, New Jersey and Delaware. Dr. Stevens also serves as Chairman of the Credentials Counsel for the Church of God in the East, District 41. He is a professional artist, a marriage counselor, and has authored all together twelve books on the subject of marriage and relationships: Marriage: Castle, Corridors, and Conflicts; Marriage: The Rules of the Game;

Marriage: Catching a Second Wind; Love, Marriage, and The Baby Carriage; Falling Back In Love; Falling Back in Love, Again; and Love, Marriage, and Your Kids. Included are 3 online books: LOVE FOR A LIFETIME; MARRIAGE FOR A LIFETIME; EQUIPPING BABIES FOR A LIFETIME, and a children's book, TIMMY'S LUNCH.

Dr. Stevens has produced various sundry videos and publications. Each week he faithfully sends out scores of email sermon outlines called Mail-A-Messages to an online congregation. He has also opened up a cyber counseling ministry through Face Book, YouTube, Instagram, and the www.soundmarriages.com website where people can get relationship counseling anonymously if desired.

Dr. Stevens is married to Mrs. Dorothy Grimball Stevens, and together they have four children all actively serving in the church at large. Dr. and Mrs. Stevens have 10 grandchildren, and 2 great grands. They co-founded the Second Wind Second Mile Ministries, now known as "Sound Marriages" over 40 years ago. Their marital philosophy is, "Making good marriages even better." Dr. & Mrs. Stevens have travelled nationwide doing seminars, presentations, workshops, and private counseling sessions, sometimes at their own expense. They say, "Because we love God and His people"! Website info:

https://www.drstevenssoundmarriages.com

www.ingramcontent.com/pod-product-compliance
Lightning Source LLC
Chambersburg PA
CBHW030256130626
46549CB00002B/564